Taste

Also by Letitia Baldrige

Etiquette

Juggling: The Art of Balancing Marriage,
Motherhood, and Career

A Lady, First: My Life in the Kennedy White House and the
American Embassies of Paris and Rome

Letitia Baldrige's Complete Guide to a Great Social Life

Letitia Baldrige's Complete Guide to Executive Manners

Letitia Baldrige's Complete Guide to the
New Manners for the 90's

Letitia Baldrige's New Complete Guide to Executive Manners

Letitia Baldrige's New Manners for New Times:
A Complete Guide to Etiquette

Of Diamonds and Diplomats

Public Affairs, Private Relations

Roman Candle

LETITIA BALDRIGE

·

Taste

·

ACQUIRING
WHAT MONEY CAN'T BUY

(T·T)

Truman Talley Books

St. Martin's Press ❧ New York

www.stmartins.com

ISBN-13: 978-0-312-35173-1
ISBN-10: 0-312-35173-9

First Edition: June 2007

10 9 8 7 6 5 4 3 2 1

*I dedicate this book to my editor and publisher,
Truman "Mac" Talley, an old friend who had the idea
for a book on taste and the courage to see it through.
A true gentleman of the old school, Mac listened with
aplomb to my shocking tales of what is happening
today in social mores and with pleasure to the
more hopeful news of tasteful environments that
continue to be created.*

CONTENTS

INTRODUCTION

ONE OF the things I really enjoyed in writing this book was asking friends, associates, and strangers of any age what the word *taste* meant to them. It is such a subjective word, and the question usually drew a perplexed look, followed by serious thinking. Then questions were tossed back to me. A sixteen-year-old boy asked for clarification: "You mean something that tastes good, like Tastee-Freez?" Obviously his thoughts went immediately to his stomach. A thirty-year-old bachelor told me, "Taste is having the good sense to wear a business shirt and tie—a good tie, not a cheap, loud one—if you're about to meet your girlfriend's parents." A young woman who had just graduated from college looked puzzled by my question, then said, "I'm too young to know anyone with real taste, but my mother said several times, 'If ever anyone had taste, it was Jackie Kennedy.'" She smiled in triumph when I said, "Good answer," like a quiz show host. Good taste to her, and hundreds of thousands like her, simply meant a woman named Jackie Kennedy.

One of my favorite definitions of taste comes from Professor Pier Massimo Forni, of Johns Hopkins University in Baltimore. A renowned writer on civility and manners, he remarked, "Someone with good taste is a member of an elite whose talent is choosing well." These good choices are made in many different areas. Some people think of taste only in terms of food. My mother viewed it entirely in terms of character: you dress respectfully so as not to offend your host. You act appropriately to show that your parents taught you how to do things tastefully, and you avoid being the "noisy child," which upsets everyone. Luckily for me, there was relief in sight from my mother's stern definition: "What you do in your own backyard is very different," she added.

Interior designers may think of taste only in terms of home decoration. Those in the fashion industry think of taste only as it pertains to their field. One wag who has been in New York's garment industry for many decades took a long sip of his gin and tonic and answered my question with three words: "Taste is restraint." Long before him, the novelist and interior designer Edith Wharton said it more poetically: "Taste expresses the mysterious demand of the eye and mind for symmetry, harmony, and order." She added her most famous quote: "The essence of taste is suitability." And later she said, "Taste is the power of producing excellence, a rejection of what is bad, and an attachment to what is better."

Elsie de Wolfe (also known as Lady Mendl), who was one of the first great women decorators in America, had a rather snooty attitude, which, of course, works: "Style is something one is born with, and the interior designer's job is to introduce new money to old furniture." In discussing the taste of some of the rich people of her time, Elsie warned, "Money talks, and it can make horrible sounds!" On another occasion she said: "Bad taste is an ingrained condition for which there is no known cure." I would disagree with her on that point: in my experience, one can develop taste through careful observation of one's environment, travel, and study of other cultures and eras.

As legendary fashion editor Edna Woolman Chase, editor in chief of *Vogue* from 1914 to 1952, once remarked, "Fashion can be purchased, but style one must possess." She was saying either you have taste or you don't, and money won't buy it, but she omitted the most important part of her philosophy: self-education will give you a sense of taste.

Every part of the world has beauty in its origins, history, and culture. From the prehistoric paintings in the caves of Europe to the giant statues on Easter Island, from the pyramids of Egypt to the mysterious rock formations at Stonehenge, and from the great temples in Indochina to the rhythmic columns of ancient Greece, there have always been examples of great beauty and artistry, natural and manmade. As a first step toward training your eye and developing taste, ask yourself why people from all over the world gasp not only at the engineering genius of the Via Appia Antica and the Roman aqueduct but also at their artistic beauty. What makes people want to stand in front of the Taj Mahal for hours, just gazing at its façade?

Philosophers, critics, and writers have traditionally related the subject of taste only to people of great wealth, but today anyone can reach for the brass ring (make that a *gold* ring) on the merry-go-round. To be able to seize the ring can affect one's life permanently and pleasantly. In this superfast civilization, where one can physically cross oceans, mountains, and boundaries in minutes, where time no longer needs to limit us, and where commerce and culture have entered the global dimension, the importance of aesthetic values is growing, rather than receding. Self-education can accomplish miracles in advancing knowledge and sophistication, and one does not have to belong to the upper class to receive these benefits. When we better ourselves, broaden our horizons, and begin to make good choices in taste, we become more interesting, tolerant human beings in the process.

I hope that the readers of this book will find the subject stimulating and rewarding, and that it will set them off on their own individual searches for the sense, spirit, aesthetics, and even the logic of good taste. Of course, each of us is justified in saying,

"Hey, my good taste is as good as your good taste anytime, so what exactly are you talking about?" It's not easy to explain exactly what anyone is talking about on this subjective, emotional topic, but it's worth exploring. Our taste is the composite of the choices we make in life, and good taste is very difficult to achieve when there are many poor choices around us. Many have said that the Victorian and post-Victorian eras were such times because darkness, heaviness, and gloom prevailed in interiors and in fashion.

The only absolute in taste is that it changes with the differences in nationality, history, exploration, international commerce, fads, customs, disasters, and wars. That adds up to a lot of changes! It is becoming harder and harder to keep up with the many variations in taste from one culture to another. To develop a sense of taste is to possess a good "eye," which means to be a sharp observer. A good eye requires researching different eras and following roads to other parts of the world. It also requires the will to learn and understand the environment around us.

Everyone seems to want taste, but few are able to summon the words to describe it. There seem to be as many definitions of it as there are people who ever bother to think about this ethereal, controversial, misunderstood, highly emotional subject. The problem is that our preferences change so often with the passage of time. Buildings, books, designs, and manners that are very popular in one generation may be perversely despised in the next. The consolation for a traditionalist is that something *démodé* this year may very well become popular again in a few decades.

Take, for example, our musical tastes. Look at the rock stars of the 1960s and 1970s, now back on tour, singing the same songs. It seems as though anyone still strong enough to hold a guitar is back in the spotlight. Or look at the new craze in ballroom dancing, and the couples swinging once again to the beat of Cole Porter's "Night and Day" and anything by George Gershwin, Jerome Kern, and Irving Berlin. *Vintage* is fashion's favorite new buzzword, and beaded Indian moccasins are back, as are old-fashioned leggings, hot oatmeal cereal, croquet, dirndl skirts, and the welcome sight of men wearing suits to work.

It's unfortunate that the word *taste* ignites such *malaise* in so many of us. We may not be able to define it, but we all want it, whatever it is, and few would ever accept the premise that we are lacking in it. "Taste is bloody hard to define," a young British rock star recently pronounced, "but we know what's on, we know what's on in our own lyrics and in our *kit,* and in what we do onstage. We never do really *naff* stuff. We do right in our performances."

There's your taste and my taste, as well as good taste and bad, and who has the right to make the call, good or bad? Frankly, an exercise of the brain is called for, and you have to put your faith in someone. There's Hispanic taste, African-American taste, Southwestern taste, and many more on the list. There's tasty, tasteless, or no-taste taste. But what exactly are we talking about anyway? Friends may build a new home—a McMansion—at great expense, yet you know you would feel uncomfortable spending the night there. Others may manage to make over a very modest dwelling into a place of warmth and charm, where you could happily move right in to stay.

The difference is that elusive, very valuable human asset, *taste;* it affects how you perceive something, how you feel about it. My mother, God bless her, thought of it in terms of behavior and character as well as beauty.

I remember when, at the age of twelve, I was the proud writer, producer, and costume coordinator of a children's neighborhood musical for the benefit of a local charity. I solved the vexing problem of how to dress the chorus of ten little girls, average age of nine, by instructing each to borrow a nightgown from her mother, which they could wear over their regular clothes. The gowns were much too long, of course, and dragged dangerously about our little stage. Proud of my resourcefulness, I purchased a box of large safety pins and had my chorus hoist up their nightgowns, pinning the skirts to their shoulders, solving the length problem and creating a waterfall effect of cascading, lace-trimmed polyester. When my mother came across the scene, she shook with laughter and immediately ordered the cast to remove their mothers' nightgowns and to forget about performing in any costume. When I demanded to know why, she said, "Because your idea, Letitia, even though you didn't realize it, resulted in a spectacle onstage of the worst possible taste, that's why."

When you hear someone referred to as "a person of great taste," you probably think first of someone who is good-looking, beautifully dressed, and most likely rich, with a snazzy car and a fabulous house (or houses). But is a great home one that is illuminated by a big dollar sign, or one where there is proof everywhere that the owner cares about the comfort and pleasure of everyone inside it? I will never forget my husband's and my visit to Winfield House, the

American ambassador's residence in London, a mansion that had recently been donated by heiress Barbara Hutton to our government. Before we left to return to the United States, Evangeline Bruce, the wife of Ambassador David Bruce, handed me a notepad and a pen. She didn't ask, but rather commanded me to write down every little thing that could be improved in the luxurious guest suite. The only thing I could think of was that the bathroom was dark (the only kind of bathroom in England in the 1950s), and therefore it was hard to put on makeup. Within a week's time, she had a new overhead chandelier installed with clear, soft bulbs, and a large illuminated makeup mirror requiring nothing more than a push of a button to work. That is what describes "a hostess with great taste" as much as her wonderful selections in decorating details.

My own take on this subject is that the underlying key to a person's taste is his or her character. A man or woman can be known and respected for good taste, regardless of job or income level, if they make good choices in clothes, have good table manners, are kind, and organize their home to look warm, welcoming, clean, and appropriate to their station in life.

People of wealth will be judged as having no taste if they are transformed into fashion victims every time they dress (such as the Hollywood actress who wears a leopard-print tunic and hot pants to match the interior of her convertible and her small dog's raincoat). People with money who own disorganized, badly designed, overly glitzy homes are far from tasteful; the case is worse if they are also loudmouths, show-offs, and people who are nasty to others. This is why taste has become a taboo subject. If you are a student of architecture, you may worship at the feet of Walter Gropius, who in his architectural designs in the 1920s heralded the oncoming revolution—the merging of functionalism and the machine aesthetic. At the same time, you may look upon Donald Trump's gilded mansion in Palm Beach, Mar-A-Lago, as "a blaze of polychrome vulgarity," to quote Stephen Bayley.

Coco Chanel always used to say that taste is the opposite of vulgarity. Palm Beach interior designer Barclay Fryery, in discussing it in terms of character, defines it as "kindness." As far as design is concerned, he calls taste a gift. "If you have a wee spark of it—it can be cultivated into something special, and it also means consistency, picking a style and sticking to it."

Mario Buatta, a New York interior designer of renown, and I used to sit and chat by the hour on the subject of taste when he was in his early years as an up-and-coming professional, and I was running my company with many home furnishings industry clients. I remember his telling me how difficult it was to persuade a wonderful young couple with money to keep their minds open and welcoming for unified, logical plans in their new home. He said it was sometimes like pulling immovable objects back and forth to open up their minds to fresh ideas, whether for wall colors or window treatments, not just the tried-and-true concepts they'd liked in the shelter magazines.

A person who has never had any education in the arts can look at Botticelli's painting *La Primavera* (Spring) and absolutely *feel* the beauty in it. When visiting someone's new house, that same uneducated person may look at a ceramic toilet bowl that has been hand-painted with a wild profusion of flowers, birds, and animals in garish colors, and judge what was meant to be a modern work of art a tasteless object. That the new house's owner paid a fortune for the toilet bowl doesn't make it any more tasteful to the beholder, perhaps less so.

The only universally accepted premise is that taste is subjective. You look at the physical world around you with a unique pair of eyes. Someone may highly praise an object that you examine and find is unremittingly vulgar. The visual bad taste hits you in the face like the stinging smack of a wet fish. The difference in individual tastes is startling. Just to illustrate this, I invited a group of women for lunch and asked each one to bring the ugliest object (not too big) she could lay her hands on, whether it was something in her closet or borrowed from her mother-in-law's closet. The only requirement: that it be ugly.

I put my horror object, which I had found in a thrift shop and purchased just for this occasion, on the corner of console table in our hall. It was a lamp, a dark pewter electrified candlestick, probably circa 1930, topped with a reproduction of a gray German World War I–type helmet, from which hung, in a slanted pattern, what looked like a long beaded curtain of strings of tiny pearls. Every movement of air would cause the beaded curtain to move, or rather to shimmy. When the ladies arrived with their objects to display on the dining-room table, to await the judging of the ugliest one, one of the chicest of the guests bubbled with enthusiasm, "Letitia, that is the most interesting-looking lamp sitting on your *demi-lune*! I have never seen anything quite like it. It's a treasure. Do you have its provenance? It's to die for!" Three of the ladies asked where they could purchase one.

Different strokes for different folks. I did not have the heart to put it on the table with the other entrants in the ugliest contest. I substituted something else, alas, not half as hideous. I have vowed never to look at the beaded curtain lamp again. Taste plays an undeniably mysterious role in our minds. Why is the eye so thoroughly engaged when beholding certain vistas or even small objects? Why does a silken robe made in Asia become so coveted in Buenos Aires, London, Stockholm, or Johannesburg? And why do people go into raptures when eating an extraordinary pasta with truffles or sipping a delicious glass of wine or attacking a dish of very good ice cream covered with a very good chocolate sauce? Life is a lot more interesting the moment that one's taste is engaged.

It is taste that makes us want to look, possess, ingest, and experience with every one of our senses everything that gives us great pleasure.

ONE

•

Just Who Is This
PERSON OF TASTE?

A PERSON acquires taste not by accident, but by spending years training his or her eye and learning how to make good judgments. It used to be easy to be labeled a "person of taste." All you had to do was be born into an old family, receive a good education at the institutions where your parents and grandparents had studied, become considered a reputable member of society, and realize that life is a product of making good—or bad—choices.

Today, it is no longer easy to achieve this plateau. We are a society in which instant celebrity rules, rather than accomplishment and standards of excellence. This means that our current role models may not be paragons of taste. At the same time, we have broken free of many traditions and customs of the past, and we are left to find our own way, often guided by dubious examples. Take, for instance, the wedding, the celebrity wedding in particular.

One always used to find taste in a great wedding because sacred, tried-and-true traditions kept the bride and groom and their families and guests from making mistakes. It was all there, in the fine print, ever since the time of Queen Victoria's wedding to Prince Albert. The first-time bride wears all white, with a chapel veil and cathedral train. Those traditions have been shattered: the bride now can wear red, kelly green, or a stripper's costume if she wishes. An enormous industry of bridal consultants with no training has sprung up to oversee the taste and pageantry of the costly event. The bride may be on her third wedding, but the customs of the long, sweeping, lacy virginal veil and the saucy garter toss to the groomsmen can still prevail. If a film star in her fifties, married a few times before, walks up the aisle this time in what can only be described as a short, filmy, pleated, transparent beige nightgown, Empire style, hold the presses. Stock the bridal stores across the country with hundreds of copies based on this design. It's an overnight sensation—the new, acceptable, "chic" style in bridal wear. The nightgown! Somewhere along the way the attribute of taste has simply vanished.

But there are still some real taste advocates out there—of all races, colors, and distinctions. Their voices will still be heard, and their influence can only become more effective as people in our society grow tired of the super hype, the loud, the garish, and the ugly. The young people in this country— those in their twenties and thirties—will make the difference. Let us put our faith in them. They are traveling and absorbing history and new ideas with their cell phones and BlackBerries turned off. They are training their eyes. And as they step into their roles as the future tastemakers of America, they would do well to cast a glance back in time and consider the contributions made by prominent tastemakers of the past, most notably Jacqueline Kennedy. We will focus this chapter on her story, for she was *the* person of taste throughout her lifetime, and her influence lingers on. As you read about her and in later chapters about other smart, stylish doyennes of taste, consider the lessons that you can draw from their lives and apply to your own.

Tasteful Interiors

Jacqueline Kennedy's brilliant gift for fashion was rivaled only by her flair for interior decoration, seen in the White House restorations. In a stroke of genius, she formed the Fine Arts Committee of the White House, consisting of prominent preservationists and millionaires. Henry du Pont, of the Winterthur estate near Wilmington, Delaware, became chairman, a curator was chosen, and the committee members were soon busy at work, overseeing the restoration and placing suitable antiques in all the public rooms.

Jackie knew the program, in order to survive, much less thrive, needed an official blessing from on high. She therefore managed to bring a most renowned figure, the doyen of the National Gallery, David Finley, onto and under the prestigious umbrella of the newly formed committee. With a man of Finley's expertise, the White House restoration projects now had the most important imprimatur they could have. Finley was a minute figure of a man with a powerhouse of a reputation, which was formed from the time he became the young assistant to the philanthropist and former secretary of the Treasury Andrew Mellon, overseeing the construction of the National Gallery of Art's great marble building and its superb collection of art. He became the guardian of Washington's cultural and historic landmarks, and was the number-one scholar of all periods of the White House. Jackie's exchange of letters with him shows the power of a woman's flattery in making an important man continue to support her project without hesitation. Feminine wiles. They are extremely useful, and one wonders if the women leaders of today, maneuvering around in the *pond* of our nation's capital, have ever used such a feminine tool to their advantage.

Jackie knew how to put the White House Historical Association together, with the help and legal advice from a host of government officials, past and present. She also knew the necessity of money, and the group therefore included a number of millionaires (billionaires by today's semantics). They felt honored to even sit in the presence of a man like David Finley, such a far cry from their Wall Street and corporate environments.

There was a public appeal for funds, but the

greatly desired big-ticket items, such as the exquisite antique Aubusson rug now in the Red Room,
were paid for from checkbooks the Fine Arts Committee members pulled out of their pockets on the
spot when money was needed. (It's the only kind of
nonprofit committee roster to have!)

The committee's adviser, Stéphane Boudin, of
the famed House of Jansen in Paris, already knew all
of the committee members. Many of them were
customers of his chic establishment in Paris. He was
an expert on nineteenth-century furnishings and the
decorative arts in general. Congress was not happy at
seeing a dapper Frenchman in charge of this very
American White House restoration program, but
Boudin managed to remain out of the headlines and
quietly do his job to perfection. He ignored the jeal-
ousies of the various design consultants attached to
the project, which was the only way to handle the
situation. He simply was "unavailable" when they
and the press were hunting him down.

The Kennedys had a strong sense of history,
which made it fascinating to watch the meticulous,
authentic restoration of the public rooms of the
White House. A deft touch was required to remove
the ugliness of past history from those historic walls

and to make the rooms lighter and brighter without sacrificing the stylistic principles of the period. The depressingly dark green, lifeless state dining room metamorphosed into a lovely space painted in three different colors of white. A famous German painter who specialized in marbleizing (he could paint any surface so that the observer could not possibly tell it was not marble) worked in the White House for weeks on end. One morning I saw that the president, on his early-morning trip over to his West Wing office, had stopped for a chat with the painter, who was up on a very tall ladder, working on the wall moldings. What began as a routine question about what the painter was doing turned into a twenty-minute conversation. JFK was a curious man, interested in everyone's life and occupation. As expected, each object of his scrutiny—particularly the everyday workers he would question—were flattered beyond belief by the presidential attention.

The president knew that Jackie's taste was expensive, and he complained about her personal bills with regularity, which made her a typical housewife, at least in that way. (Probably in no other way.) More important than her overspending, however, was the fact that her husband basked in the attention and praise she attracted, even from America's cultural intellectuals. He was smart enough never to be jealous of her popularity because a lot of it rubbed off on him, too.

The First Lady realized that the tourists tramping through the public rooms of the White House did not have a clue about American history or nineteenth-century design, so she helped start the White House Historical Association and pushed the members to publish the first official guidebook for the White House. Each administration from then on updated it and added an explanation of their own changes and gifts to the house. The sale of the guidebook has helped cover the enormous cost of the upkeep of the house.

Jackie further instructed the public on White House history when she hosted a CBS televised tour of the newly refurbished and restored building. Working without a script, she wandered from room to room, telling the history of the furniture, paint colors, portraits, and great paintings on loan from various museums. It was seen over and over by millions of people. A trip to Washington to see the White House very quickly became the number-one travel destination of the American public.

The Private Quarters

Celebrated New York decorator Sister Parish and her young partner, Albert Hadley, were invited by Mrs. Kennedy to oversee the redesign of the family quarters upstairs. Sister, a family friend who had known Jackie from the time she was a child, was considered a maverick for working so hard in the decorating field when she was a member of one of America's most prominent families. She followed in the tradition of Edith Wharton and Elsie de Wolfe Mendl as a woman outstanding in her field who was criticized for "working," a most unfeminine activity! The family floor above the public rooms of the White House proved to be a challenge since the entire rabbit warren of rooms had to be redone, including the creation of a cheerful little girl's room for Caroline and a baby boy's room suitable for John. New closets had to be arranged in the existing space, because no First Lady since Dolley Madison had had a wardrobe quite like Jacqueline Kennedy's.

The first White House hairdressing salon was constructed in a corner on the family floor, spawning great professional rivalry for the position of "First Coiffeur," a title of immeasurable esteem in the beauty world. Jackie's chestnut brown hair, thick and lustrous, was the envy of everyone who saw her. But what shocking news to hear that there was a hair salon on the sacred premises of our president's home! Soon Alexandre de Paris was considered her official hairdresser when Jackie was in Europe, and Kenneth Battelle of New York was considered her official hairdresser when she was in the United States. While under the hair dryer she managed to work through a mass of decorating details of the White House restoration. The hairdresser's various products and Jackie's file folders were merged in perfect harmony in that historic little White House room.

TWO

•

Good Taste in
FASHION

*S*USAN SONTAG, the late critic and analyst of arts, ideas, and society, once wrote that "Intelligence is a kind of taste—a taste of ideas." What is unfair is that some people are just born with the ephemeral talent of pulling themselves together in an attractive way before appearing in public.

Bon vivant and society writer of nineteenth-century England Oscar Wilde gave fashion an important nod when he said, "One should either be a work of art, or wear a work of art." That's an important statement. Mothers with great style don't automatically pass on these genes to their daughters, although living with family members who have wonderful taste can successfully train a child's eye. But an individual of any age or background who constantly uses his or her eyes to observe and seeks to understand just why this man or that woman is "lookin' good" is developing a sense of taste.

Some of us don't care if we're grungy-looking and badly dressed, as if to thumb our noses at the establishment. Some of us lead lives where casual dress makes sense most of the time. Following fashion wisely is a lot of work—brain work, in fact, involving planning skills, a good sense of timing, and an understanding of what *appropriate* means. It also involves money. In justification for the extra work and expense, there are compelling advantages in being considered by peers, associates, bosses, and lovers as someone who dresses well.

A woman can be dressed in style and yet be badly dressed. On the other hand, she can be dressed without any formality, in slacks and a sweater, and because of the way she puts it all together, the result makes a statement of great style.

The conspicuous minority that instinctively dresses

with taste always stands out in a crowd. They constitute an attractive part of the scenery. They are also propelled forward in business and social life. People want to have them around, to be seen in their company. They are considered sophisticated and knowledgeable.

Of course, there are many things more important than fashion. An elderly pillar of Boston society once told me, "I don't care how any of these young people at my party are dressed, as long as they *smell clean!*"

Many agree with those who don't really care about fashion and personal appearance, sincerely believing there's so much more of greater import in life. And, of course, they are right. Or perhaps they just want to fit in anywhere inconspicuously, with no distinct air of fashion about them. It's the "I just don't want anyone to notice whether or not I'm here" attitude that makes that person unobjectionable, no matter what he or she is wearing. Unobjectionable, yes, but also forgettable, perhaps even invisible.

It is a glorious fact that many men and women with a good fashion sense have the ability to live within their budget. They buy wisely and well. They buy classics, and accessories that coordinate with their color scheme. They make good, careful choices in their clothes, their grooming is impeccable, and the aura of their appearance is one of taste.

You may be one of those many women who not only wants to look good but wants to excel in your physical image. You get a great rush from standing above the crowd in quality of attire, hairstyle, makeup, jewelry, accessories, including the briefcase and handbag you carry, and, of course, the car you drive, the kind of garden you tend, and the breed of dog you may or may not cherish.

Status symbols, yes, they are all that, but when we use them with restraint (and really love our dog), and when we don't fall victim to the obnoxious disease of total dependency on designer logos, we can project self-confidence. We feel we look as good as we can because we have made the right selections for any event, at any time of day, and in any kind of climate.

Paris Copies

Some people are very label-conscious. The store, the designer name, even the fabric is snob-important.

I'm reminded of the late Vala Byfield in the 1950s, a stunning Hungarian married at that time to Ernie Byfield Jr. in New York. She was a member of the International Best Dressed List, but was more famous for her enormous diamond solitaire, the size of a Ping-Pong ball.

"I don't have to buy zee insurance," she said proudly, "because zee ring is nervaire off me. When I take a bath, my ring does, too. If a thief thinks he gets my ring, he will have to saw off my finger, and zat takes a veery long time to do. He won't have zee time!"

Then, in New York, a flood of very handsome copies of French couture dresses and suits made their way into the less expensive stores in New York, such as Alexander's, Macy's, and Orbach's. The copies were remarkably well done and sold in those days for around one hundred dollars for a daytime dress, while the French original would sell for three thousand. It became "the thing to do" for rich American clotheshorses to wear these copies and brag about it.

One night the Byfields gave a cocktail party for a few friends before a black-tie benefit dinner dance. We all complimented Vala on her beautiful Dior ballgown copy, but then another guest arrived wearing the exact same dress from Orbach's. Before five minutes had passed, Vala had changed into another beautiful dress, saying she had accidentally spilled red wine down the front of her Dior copy. Later on, by chance I saw the label in her dress, which had been thrown on her bed. The label was not Orbach's. It read CHRISTIAN DIOR. She had bought the original in Paris and had been proudly passing it off as an Orbach's copy!

Reverse chic, one might say.

On occasion, one accessory can result in the success of a person's entire look. When I was invited by the Finnish government to address the country's home-furnishings manufacturers on the subject of America's "Contract Furniture Market," in the new architecturally splendid Alvar Aalto hall in Helsinki, my hosts surprised me afterward with a generous gift certificate to Finland's major fur salon. The gift was comparable to inviting a child to visit Santa's display center at the North Pole. I immediately availed myself of an oversized, slouchy chinchilla beret, the most luxurious fur in existence in that era. Once back in the United States I was constantly granting permission to people who wanted to touch my beret; it was a sensual thrill to anyone whose fingers moved over the soft, opulent texture of the skins.

In 1970, no one had ever owned a more beautiful, glamorous, or visually spectacular hat. Twelve years later, after I had worn that beret in the thick of winter with tailored suits, sweaters, brocaded evening suits, and even ski jackets, it went to its final resting place in a thrift shop, but only after I had bade it a fond and grateful farewell. It was the most elegant speaker's fee I ever received, as well as having served as my most enduring and endearing accessory success!

In the early years of postwar Paris, when visiting American tourists stopped me on the street to ask for directions, I could tell in advance where they were headed: the Chanel and Christian Dior boutiques. The general opinion was that any fragrance or cosmetic product with either label just "had to be good." And, of course, there was Jean Patou for perfume and Hermès for bags and scarves. The cult of the "snob label" had arrived in America. The great old prewar French houses experienced a rebirth as far as the outside world was concerned. It was fascinating to watch. Beautiful salons like Guerlain and Jacques Fath suddenly reopened their doors in the depressed postwar environment. Chic women from all over Western Europe suddenly reappeared in the place Vendôme, on the rue Royale, the avenue Montaigne, and the avenue Franklin Roosevelt.

Mrs. David Bruce was courted by all of the houses because when *Harper's Bazaar* photographed her wearing one of Madame Grès's signature pleated jersey designs, or when she was photographed in a

Jean Desses chiffon evening dress, draped across a Louis XV sofa in the living room of the embassy residence, the Paris *salons de couture* could not accommodate the number of women from all over the world who immediately wanted the same dresses, even if they had to order them at an outrageous premium through a high-priced local store like Marshall Field's of Chicago, Joseph Horne of Detroit, Bergdorf Goodman of New York, G. Fox of Hartford, Burdines of Palm Beach, or Neiman Marcus of Dallas. American women languished with unrequited love for anything from Paris. Then the slumbering giant of Italian couture, its sportswear in particular, awoke with a start, anxious for some of the riches flowing so freely into the beauty and fashion industries in France. Fashion slumbered no more. It had awakened from the war.

"What You Wear Is a Matter of Taste, but So Is What You Don't Wear"

Fashion really began in prehistoric times when the cavewomen selected one set of animal skins over another for their body coverings, after the men did the killing. Or perhaps the women did most of the hunting and cutting of skins. In any case, someone made choices among the hides that the animal kingdom could provide. Beyond the realm of practicality, namely warmth and protection from the climate, taste was exercised when it came to the beauty of the skins.

Native Americans had their own sophisticated fashion trade as they worked their animal skins, adorning them with feathers, beads, and embroidery. They also painted their faces and bare skin with artistic skill, particularly when they were going into battle. We know how fashion conscious they were just by looking at the paintings of Native American life in museums today. In stark contrast, we've also seen paintings of the Pilgrims and early colonists in America, dressed in plain, rough clothing suitable for a life of physical labor and strict religious observance.

In the same era, a very different fashion climate existed in Europe. When Louis XIV made beauty and fashion almost mandatory for the French court, foreign visitors went home wide-eyed from viewing the splendors of Versailles, probably vowing to have a little of that in their own lives, too. The reputation of French fashion was launched. By the time Benjamin Franklin returned from his period of diplomatic service in France, he was besieged by other

American officials and friends wanting to know "what the French courtiers, men and women, are wearing now."

Next to Versailles, the English royal courts were probably the runners-up in arousing international fashion interest, with the Spanish, Italian, and Dutch courts following quickly behind. One has only to inspect the museum portraits of well-known figures in every part of the world to notice that the subjects are dressed in their very best. Even in the courtyards of the provincial farms, that "very best" was handsome.

It seems that since the seventeenth century, other nations have been jealous of French fashion: it is hardly in the best national interests of a nation to allow the fashion superiority of another country to undermine their own countries' creative efforts and marketing activity.

The French held on to the Western world fashion lead well into the 1900s. Since the days when the first trading vessels laden with the finest linens, cotton, silks, and velvets made their rounds from country to country, the best-quality fabrics either remained behind on the French shores or were exported from them, carried by ships to other countries under the French imprimatur. Among the rich and the royal, taste was recognized by anyone with a discerning eye. The brisk trade in dress and upholstery fabrics saw the accompanying rise of the trimming industry in France. Needlework, including exquisite laces, ribbons, and embroideries, was eagerly exchanged among countries, to the delight of anyone with the good sense to realize that these trimmings made beautiful things that much more beautiful.

As shown in the paintings of major artists like Watteau and Fragonard, court life in the days of the French Louis kings was a pastel world of pretty pinks and pale blues, but thanks to the Far East, there were other color influences, such as bright reds, too. A pair of male courtier's pumps is described in an advertisement of the late 1600s as made of "honey-colored oriental silk, lined in bright blue taffeta." The art of the period reflected the establishment of fashion as a serious industry. You have only to peruse the images made by the painters and sketchers of their lavishly attired seventeenth- and eighteenth-century subjects to realize that millions of hours of handwork and large fortunes had been required for the extravagant attire of the royals and the dandies of that world.

Women from London to St. Petersburg anxiously awaited the news of Paris trends, so they could copy them. The standards of taste were dictated by the French, even if the designers for the royal courts of England and Western Europe proudly began to take their places in the sun. After witnessing the success of Worth, Poiret, and Charles James abroad, American designers began to emerge in the beginning of the twentieth century, neatly tying into the growth of America's new "society-cum-large-fortune" population.

The Hair on One's Head

When I was a little girl, my grandmother gave me a framed pair of pastel lithographs of Louis XVI and Marie Antoinette. They have hung over my bed all of these years, reminding me of the absolutely wondrous life of the French royals. Marie's portrait is amazing for its clear image of her dress, billowing forth like a waterfall over wide panniers of cascading flounces of lace and bows. But it is her wig, with an artistry of bows adorning it, that makes the eye linger on all this magnificence.

By the late seventeenth century, elaborate new wig styles (overrun with false curls and extensions) were part of the arduous process of getting dressed to attend a court event. No fuss over today's Academy Awards night could approach these court appearances. Everyone in France who followed fashion knew the names of the leading hairstylists.

Louis XIV had his own wig room at Versailles. Some of the concoctions reached absurd, towering heights, serving as theatrical stages for models of ships at full sail, miniature royal gilded coaches, and miniature still-life paintings of fruits, flowers, and food, any of which managed to be tucked into a wig. The ladies must have exemplified the term *top-heavy* and have had a terrible time entering their covered coaches with wigs looking like complete stage sets! Their escorts must have had to ride in separate carriages.

The business of buying and selling wig hair was brisk in the seventeenth and eighteenth centuries. Strands had to be twenty-four inches long in order to fit into the wig designers' schemes, and the favored color was ash blond. The cost of wig hair was prohibitive. One pound of it would require a seventeenth-century courtier to pay the equivalent of $7,500, which in today's terms would be several hundred thousand dollars.

By the 1660s the word *coiffeur* had come into France's vocabulary. A *coiffeur* (or a *coiffeuse,* as a woman hairdresser was called) was inevitably French. The man who in the 1600s filled the position that

Alexandre de Paris would later fill as Jacqueline Kennedy's celebrated hairdresser was a much-talked-about womanizer named Monsieur Champagne. Women waited for months to see him, and he took as clients only women of high birth, great fortune, and enormous sex appeal.

The wig craze continued well into the eighteenth century, but in 1671, the trendsetting women at the French court cut their hair short and wore it curly. There was a momentary fashion cry of "no more big hair," which practically caused a riot (just like the one that Coco Chanel's cropped hair and boyish silhouette incited in the 1920s). When one stops to consider the amount of time a seventeenth-century woman had to spend on her toilette before appearing at court, it is enough to make one wonder why she got out of bed at all.

Footwear and Fashion

Shoe fetishes were also common in the birthplace of fashion, the royal courts of France. Again, Louis XIV was to blame. He was very proud of his own *jolies jambes* (pretty legs). He had fine new styles of shoes made for himself, including high-heeled mules covered in pearls, with lacy, jeweled buckles and velvet bows; this style has reemerged as a big fad in the twenty-first century. Louis XIV's courtiers immediately copied the jeweled shoes, and so did the rulers of other countries around the world. The Sun King was so shoe crazy that he forbade the wearing of boots at court, except for hunting, because they offended his eye.

Another new craze inspired by the king was for decorated heels on shoes. French artists would paint small original works on the high heels of the royal slippers. Naturally a fad followed. A lot of time was spent in foot gazing in those days. It was considered sexual sport for the male courtiers to perform feats of athleticism in order to catch a glimpse of a lady's ankle and foot as she lifted her skirts to alight from a carriage or to cope with a grandiose staircase. Her lower appendages were considered extremely erotic, and the mere suggestion of creamy, stockinged limbs under all those skirts drove men to distraction, but any man who dared to bestow a kiss on a lady's foot in public was considered a dangerous pervert. There were famous *bottiers* in France—the Manolo Blahniks and the Jimmy Choos of the day—who took full advantage of the rage for ladies' footwear.

Through the years "shoe news" continued to

come mainly from Paris, although Italian shoes moved into the style limelight after World War II.

The shortage of shoe leather during that war caused hardship to the chic young women, even if some improvised quite well.

Jacqueline Blanche arrived at Vassar when I was there in the early '40s. She was in essence a French refugee, and was, of course, amazingly chic, even though she had practically nothing in her suitcase. Her only shoes were high-heeled cork and canvas wedgies, the only kind of footwear easily available in wartime. The French went to Portugal to avail themselves of the never-ending supply of cork for the soles of women's shoes. It's ironic that cork-soled canvas shoes are today the height of American fashion for summer, retailing from celebrated shoe designers for several hundred dollars a pair.

Was It Always French?

Since the days of Louis XIV's court at Versailles, the art of dressing began and ended with Paris. American women closely followed the dictates of whatever was happening in Paris until their own designers became good enough to stand on their own—and then some.

For decades Charles Frederick Worth was the first designer name to come to the minds of American women. In the days of the Second Empire (1852–70) he made almost nothing but white dresses because that was the fashion, but during his long, illustrious career, he would forever change the way women dressed. In the 1860s he then made popular the somber tones of purple and garnet. He was one of the first designers to make geometric cuts and to use bands of lace trimmings and rows of chenille fringe, all of which required great skill. He brought attention to ladies' rear ends with his saucy evening gown bustles. He made *passementerie,* or jet embroidery, something craved by every stylish woman, and launched the popularity of large-patterned fabrics. There was security in going to a designer like Worth because good taste was assured in everything attached to his name.

Worth knew how to endear himself to his clientele. A perfectionist, he served pâté de foie gras and Madeira wine during fittings, but the craftiest idea of all was to make mannequins with the same measurements as his customers, whether they were fat or thin, so that when the house was working on the new garments, the seamstresses could fit them directly on the bodies that would wear them, without having to put up with later client fittings. Worth's sons and grandsons continued his business, and they are credited with bringing the best of men's tailoring techniques, copied from the English, to Worth's very French *maison de couture*. Jeanne Paquin helped France stay dominant in the fashion world by dressing queens, duchesses, and the richest men's mistresses in original, much discussed fashions from 1890 to 1930. By 1907 Madeleine Vionnet was making her mark by designing clothes that freed women's bodies from corsets.

The house created by Jeanne Lanvin became popular in 1890. She made mother-and-daughter dresses popular, using as her inspiration the great painters of the day, among them Vuillard, Renoir, and Fantin-Latour.

Paul Poiret made his mark on the couture world from 1908 until 1914. He caused a revolution by designing pants for women. His designs banished the rigid hourglass silhouette. Poiret's slender, long, straight dresses became the rage, showing Russian and oriental influences. I remember finding a Poiret evening dress in a box of my grandmother's clothes from her Paris days. She generously and unwisely gave me her old trunk from the attic for dress-up purposes when my friends came to play. One of many different gowns in the trunk, the Poiret was made of a silvery, clinging fabric, and my young schoolgirl friends and I vied for the privilege of strutting around in it, carrying my grandmother's big ostrich-feathered fan as an accessory. We didn't have costume museums in those days, so the Poiret ended up in the trash, as did all the rest of my grandmother's dresses, ruined by her careless granddaughter and her friends at play. If only I had known then what I know now!

Poiret was considered a prophet because he created gowns such as the one called Delphos, made of Fortuny fabric and based on the fluid drapery found in the Greek sculpture. Designer Mary McFadden scored a great triumph in the 1960s by designing ethereal evening gowns of light, pleated Fortuny fabrics, all modern versions of Poiret's Delphos gown.

Other great shooting stars of the Paris fashion scene, such as Jean Patou and Vionnet, inspired American designers like Mainbocher, Charles James, and Norman Norell. The smart Paris designers introduced their own perfumes and eventually made more money on fragrance than on haute couture. Poiret asked the artist Raoul Dufy to design perfume bottles for him as well as fabrics.

I used to watch Clare Boothe Luce with fascination when, at the embassy in Rome, she would mix two-thirds Joy perfume by Patou with one-third Petit-Pois de Senteur perfume by Caron to make the most delicious (and expensive) fragrance I had ever savored. In those days it was not unusual for a woman to mix her perfumes into her own signature scent. Clare Luce always used a generous amount of strong perfume, so that one always knew, in passing through Roman salons at large parties, whether or not the American ambassador had arrived. Many of us tried to copy her, but it was an expensive habit.

The goddess of French fashion in this era was, of course, Coco Chanel. She began by making hats in 1910, having been set up in business by a rich English lover. Her straw boaters, trimmed with ribbon and lace, created a sensation—they were so new and simple. Then she opened her first dress shop in Deauville, making loose-fitting, casual clothes that were perfect for the sporty milieu of that famous French resort. The atmosphere of the yachting society caused her to produce berets, sailor's blouses and pants, and striped maillots. When she watched her lover, Boy Capel, play polo, she began to make very chic clothes in utilitarian fabrics—wool flannel blazers and wool jersey sporty outfits. Everything she designed made her female customers look *young*. She became famous throughout the world for launching the fashion of skirt-and-sweater ensembles, two-toned pumps, backless shoes with dark leather toes, the popularity of the color beige, short skirts, bobbed hair, the beret with a clip on it, enamel and jeweled bracelets, and yards of oriental and also fake pearls, mixed with gold chains set with green and red stones. She was the first woman designer to bring out a perfume under her own name. She is credited with making suntans popular with women, who had previously hidden from the sun under large hats and umbrellas. In World War I, she brought soft, untailored suits into fashion, with straight, knee-length skirts and walking pleats that made it easy to take quick, purposeful strides. These delightfully colored, lightweight wool suits then began to appear with different colors of braided trim, and they soon became a desired acquisition of well-dressed women throughout the world. They remain popular today in spite of the inexpensive knockoffs that never seem to cease, and the expensive contemporary versions by other designers.

Chanel gave us "the little black dress." How many women today have not had one in their closets, the answer to any fashion dilemma for evening? The fabrics and colors of her suits and coats would change, but the magic persisted in the details such as brass lion-headed buttons, blouses of the same fabric as the jacket lining, and the touch of a black or white camellia on the jacket. Her two-toned pumps and slingbacks were another classic design success. She slung gold chains at the waist of her skirts. Her quilted leather shoulder bags with chain handles have persisted in style even now, in the first decade of a new century.

Chanel did not stint on lavish costumes for evening, using velvets, metallic brocades, and sequined silks. One cannot describe her influence on the whole world of fashion without spotlighting her accessories. She often wore her jewelry *en masse,* in other words, plenty of it, and equally in daylight and nighttime. The jewelry was sometimes real, sometimes costume. She had the courage to mix it all up—ivory bangles, gold charm bracelets, corals, rubies, and diamond and platinum bracelets. And lots and lots of long pearl necklaces. Women of great fashion sense have always been proud of their ability to put it all together—namely, the costume, hat, jewelry, shoes, belts, and scarves. With Chanel, they learned to leave all of the choices of elements up to her, because her sense of taste was indestructible, unchallengeable. I have seen women of fashion fame absolutely refuse to appear in a new Chanel costume, because their new Chanel pumps had not yet arrived.

Chanel also launched the pearl earring vogue—that is, she reignited a trend that had begun more than two centuries earlier with Vermeer's portrait *Girl with a Pearl Earring*. Typical of her refusal to be pedestrian, Chanel's first pair of costume jewelry pearl earrings offered to the public featured one black and one white.

After a long life of unsurpassed productivity and success, Coco Chanel died, and Karl Lagerfeld was appointed to carry on the spirit and traditions of her house. Her great taste had been uniquely her own. She unconsciously taught millions of women how to put themselves together tastefully, even if it was just to add a simple white Peter Pan collar to a white blouse and perhaps to pin a simple white camellia to it. So simple, pure, and totally feminine.

Belle of the Ball?

At last it happened. I was going to my first Paris ball, at the fabled Pré Catalan in the Bois de Boulogne. My escort, a Brit, was taller than I was and had his own white tie and tails. It was an auspicious beginning.

My dress had to be custom-made by a French seam-stress because there was nothing to fit a tall woman in all of Paris in those days. Thanks to my Vassar friend Jacqueline Blanche, I had purchased at an absurdly low price ten meters of pale blue brocaded satin. Jacqueline's husband, Hilaire Colcombet, was the owner of Bucol, the biggest luxury silk fabric house in France. There I was, with a sensational fabric, in a Marie Antoinette blue, so reminiscent of the framed portrait of her in my bedroom. I was going to fulfill a two-decade fantasy of having a ballgown like Marie Antoinette's! The night of the ball, everyone complimented me.

When I came back to Washington for Christmas, I proudly tried it on, realizing I had never really looked at myself in the dress in Paris. Mother pro-nounced the fabric perfectly exquisite, but "more fit to cover a sofa than you." Feeling crushed and de-fensive, I pressed her to continue.

"The design of your ballgown, tight at a nonslim waist, and then billowing out over those ample hips of yours is like a sailboat going before the wind." My mother, who never minced words, had likened me to a sofa and a sailboat, but in doing so, she taught me a valuable lesson. Assembling wonderful elements doesn't do it. Size, fit, and appropriateness are all essential to style. One should dress to disguise one's imperfections, not magnify them.

It was a lesson learned.

Without Good Grooming, There Is No Fashion

Some people are naturals in their adherence to good grooming. Others pride themselves on what they can get away with, without it being noticed. One woman might forgo her appointment with the colorist at the beauty salon, thinking it doesn't matter if her dark roots are showing to the point that her hair is the color of burned toast and orange marmalade. One man might decide he doesn't have time to clean and shine his mud-splashed shoes at home, and he forgets to take care of it with a wet paper towel in the men's room when he reaches the office. He hasn't been to the barber for a long time, and his hair and mustache are scruffy. Another woman doesn't worry about the soup stain on her blouse because she's wearing a scarf that she feels will cover it. Another woman, who has misapplied her makeup in a terrible rush, forgets to check a mirror when she reaches her destination. These lapses detract from a person's overall image; even the best clothes cannot compensate for negligent grooming.

Speaking of grooming, I remember well when a famous TV star and businesswoman came to a state dinner at the White House given by President and Mrs. Clinton. She was wearing a brand-new designer outfit, but it was the wrong season (pink silk shantung culottes in the dead of winter!), and the top, a white cotton shirt, had very visible traces of a light tan-colored makeup on the collar, which she could not have missed if she had bothered to look into a mirror. It obviously didn't matter to her. No matter how much that outfit may have cost, her new designer creation was a fashion disaster in a White House full of ladies floating around in beautiful winter-season evening gowns.

Tasteful Mouth

We are in a new era of dazzling white teeth, or perhaps it should be called the Era of the Smile. Sometimes we take the well-groomed mouth to extremes, however, such as when we are seen in public constantly ingesting breath mints and casually squirting all around the inside of our mouths with an atomizer, to achieve the nirvana of good breath.

The application of lipstick in public, particularly at the table in a restaurant, has long been a sore point with etiquette writers. My take on it is that it is permissible to do it quickly at the table, at the end of the meal, when everyone has finished eating. (Time: ten seconds). There are two unforgivable sins: lipstick on teeth and outside the woman's mouth outline.

Products for women's lips are a multimillion-dollar industry with guaranteed obsolescence. There are new colors every year, as well as products to keep the lips from becoming dry and cracked. There's vitamin-injected lipstick, anti-chap lipcare, lipstick remover, lip balm, lip liner, lip gloss, and the product itself—liquid or dry, matte or glossy, running the gamut in colors from an almost colorless pale Pink Camellia to a strong Purple Passion and to a quite black Ebony Parfait. The way a woman wears lipstick affects the perceptions others have of her. She may wear none at all, which brands her as the natural, sporty, outdoor type. Or she may slather it on so thick that her lips look immovable, in which case she qualifies for the title of "tart mouth," which is no compliment. For years women have asked me, in the Q&A section of my lectures, what a woman can do about the problems of lipstick when it comes to eating foods like crab legs, corn on the cob, and spareribs. The lipstick manufacturers make bold promises about their products, but unless you cement your lipstick to your lips, it is bound to smear at a barbecue. If you're in a situation where messy lipstick would be embarrassing, the solution is to refrain from eating that kind of food in front of people you want to impress. Or, before eating, you can remove all of your lipstick carefully, out of sight of any guests. When you're having lunch with your company's board of directors, being interviewed for a position, or meeting your future in-laws for the first time, common sense reminds you not to eat corn on the cob, a gooey pizza, or a man-sized submarine sandwich you can't even get your mouth around! When people talk about a person of taste, they never have any negative remarks about that individual's table manners, even while picnicking on the grass or consuming hot dogs in the bleachers at the game.

Excess Shopping in the Family

A woman of fashion taste knows how to handle a daughter whose entire life is wrapped around the shopping pole, festooned with gay ribbons, beads, sweaters of every color and length, tops of every color, fabric, and decoration, and an array of footwear that would rival the inventory of the former first lady of the Philippines, Imelda Marcos.

One woman I know became very worried about finances because her husband had made some unwise investments. She made her sixteen-year-old daughter save her apparel shopping receipts for four weeks and had her total them. She then handed the girl the published costs of a college education. Next came a list of needs furnished by a charity in which the mother is active, whose purpose is to help young girls with their education, health, and self-esteem.

"As you can see, your fashion expenditures have gotten completely out of hand," the mother told her daughter. "And since your father and I are funding all this, I suggest you rethink your budget. Either go in the direction of earning money that will go toward college, or cut down on your clothing and makeup expenses by a large amount. In any case, because of your father's and my situation, I hope you will think before spending any money in the future that is not money you have made yourself. We are not as financially secure as we used to be, and it is our fault for not having restrained this perpetual spending spree sooner."

Her approach worked, and after a few months of the daughter's woe-is-me, the spending sprees ended, much to the delight of the mother's organization devoted to helping young women in need.

Some people seem to be born with an ephemeral talent for pulling themselves together before an event with a pleasing, even exciting visual result. Even on an ordinary morning, your appearance upon leaving the house can have importance in your life. For example, one woman goes out looking loosely pulled together, like a piece of knitting with a few dropped stitches. She may be aware of her impression of sloppiness, even a little embarrassed by it. She knows she should have paid more attention to her appearance, but time was against her. For starters, she should have checked the state of her nail polish (it's chipped) the first thing that morning, but she did not. She may make a bad impression on a client as a result, or perhaps someone who is planning an important party may consider her too dowdy-looking for the event. Those who look at her closely will probably sense some sign of her discomfort because the woman is haphazardly assembled and knows it. It is not a great way for her to start her day!

Another woman will leave her home that same morning tightly pulled together, exuding perhaps even a primness. Her appearance is a finished one, from top to toe. She is the kind who thinks ahead, laying out everything the night before so that she can immediately correct possible mistakes (a stain, a tear in a seam, a skirt hem coming undone, a hole in her pantyhose, a missing button). Any one of these would be sufficient to ruin the good impression she wants to make. She leaves the house with her hair and makeup in perfect order. If she goes to the gym, she allots enough time to put herself back in order again before arriving at the office. Every article of clothing sits nicely in place on her and is in good condition, even if the outfit and the shoes are one or two seasons old. She keeps protesting that she doesn't have time for all this, yet, magically, she finds it. She has become an expert juggler.

.　　.　　.

I feel privileged to have known so many women of great fashion taste. The one thing they all had in common was the fact that they were not known solely for fashion. They were known for their talent, their brains, their contributions to society. Wearing great clothes simply made them all the more precious to their adoring public.

La Luce

Ambassador Clare Boothe Luce, my boss in Italy, was a spectacularly beautiful woman, with a magnificent pale complexion, sea blue eyes, and a head that always made her look as though she walked around with her own angelic halo attached. Her jewels were spectacular, and she had a magnificent wardrobe to match. There was one major problem, however. She didn't wear her clothes. They wore her.

Because of problems of fit, they sometimes hung almost apart from her body. She hated fittings, found them totally tiresome and unnecessary, and consequently hardly ever stood still for them. She would often ask friends to stand in for her. When she was the United States ambassador to Italy, she used her personal maid, Gretel, to fill in for her at all the fittings except perhaps the final one, at the celebrated couture houses of Eleanora Garnett, Alberto Fabiani, Irene Galitzine, the Fontana sisters, and the new young man on the scene in those days, Valentino.

I would carefully record her dictated instructions. "Tell Fabiani to make my dress three inches shorter than he would for Gretel, one inch wider in the shoulders, two inches wider in the hips," and so on. Gretel was three inches taller than the ambassador, skinny, flat-chested, and round-shouldered. The two women's measurements could not have been more disparate, but those designers were exceedingly clever. They were desperate to make couture creations for La Luce and forced her to acquiesce to "one final fitting" at which *l'ambasciatrice* herself was present, after which the finished dress, suit, or coat was delivered within twenty-four hours. After this joke of a "final fitting" (really the only fitting), the couturier would return to his atelier, take the garment completely apart at the seams, and then sew it up all over again, according to her actual measurements. It was sleight-of-hand wizardry.

"We would do anything for the privilege of dressing this famous, brilliant woman!" the couturiers said. (The fact that she was the most photographed woman in diplomatic life, with a husband, Henry Luce, who was the world's preeminent publisher, were compelling reasons for putting up with the idiosyncracies of this client.) It was a testimony to her popularity that the movie stars of the time (such as Gina Lollobrigida, Sophia Loren, and Anna Magnani) were not considered even close in importance to Clare Boothe Luce in the Italians' attitudes. She honored them by wearing clothes by their own designers. But as one *ministro* remarked, in true Italian fashion, "She is such a beautiful woman, who is noticing her clothes? Look at that face. Those eyes!"

Jackie's Fashion Taste

If ever anyone was born with taste, it was Jacqueline Bouvier Kennedy Onassis, and also her sister, Lee Bouvier. Jackie was incapable of looking messy, disheveled, or sloppy. She was inevitably pulled together, whether wearing a sweater and skirt in her school days or an elaborate, bejeweled ball gown with matching coat in her White House days.

Whether she was jumping up and down on the family trampoline in a pair of pants (always well cut!) in the "backyard" (South Lawn) of the White House or seated stiffly in the front row of the opera box of President Charles de Gaulle in Paris, regal in a one-shouldered gown by couturier Yves St. Laurent, friends or onlookers would agree that she looked "smashing, simply smashing!"

When she was "on stage," performing presidential wifely duties, that thick head of chestnut brown hair was always infuriatingly perfect. On our foreign travels, the other women around her (her Kennedy sisters-in-law and myself included) often looked as though we had just emerged from a steamy jungle or perhaps a wind tunnel, but she was perfect.

The simpler the designer gown, the more difficult it is to copy, and Jackie's originals were famous for their utter simplicity, making them quite impossible to copy successfully. Yet her fans were determined to imitate every element of her wardrobe, lingerie included. One woman sent twenty-two Butterick dress patterns, asking Mrs. Kennedy to mail them back, letting her know which one most resembled her famous Oleg Cassini sleeveless shift dresses, so she could make it for herself.

Men also wrote Jackie, inquiring about JFK's

brand of cigars so that they could brag about smoking them. In that case we said no, without revealing the real reason why: they were illegally imported Cuban cigars. Another request we denied: women's inquiries about what brand of underwear the president wore—they wanted to purchase the same kind for their husbands for Christmas.

Women told their decorators to duplicate the heavy yellow silk damask draperies with multicolored silk braided tiebacks in the East Room, and, of course, they wanted a copy of the design of the plantings in the Rose Garden, "because the same design would look well in our backyard."

Women wrote asking what Jackie ate for breakfast, how many times a day she exercised, and what her shoe size was. (That we did not divulge, in the realm of "overly personal." It was 10B.) Eavesdroppers would pick up bits of her conversation in restaurants and release them to the press. My staff and I were forced to spend so much time and effort answering her mail and fending off unwelcome invaders of her privacy that I felt like a defender of the realm.

Women who had never been on a horse and who never would mount a horse suddenly began wearing riding breeches during the day, with any kind of boot they could find, including snowboots. The fact that Mrs. Kennedy "looked so good in jodhpurs" while photographed riding in Virginia was reason enough.

Jacqueline Kennedy deserves a special place in history. She epitomized the broadest definition of the word *taste*, encompassing the fields of entertaining, conversation, interior design, intelligence, and beautiful manners. For every gift, every lunch or dinner she attended, she either wrote notes by hand or had me draft thank-you notes for her signature. When it was someone she did not know, my Social Office would write "on behalf of Mrs. Kennedy to thank you for your beautiful flowers" (or "thoughtful gift" or whatever it was). Every single item was acknowledged, except when the president was assassinated; then the outpouring of letters, cards, and flowers overwhelmed the White House. (When this happened, Mrs. Kennedy had her social secretary, Nancy Tuckerman, arrange for notes to be sent, but she also went on television a couple of times to express her public gratitude for the millions of letters, flowers, messages, masses, and prayers offered up for her husband.)

Jackie wrote notes of encouragement to friends who were hospitalized, and letters of congratulations to friends when their babies were born or when their children achieved some kind of honor, scholastic or otherwise. Her notes were charming and were indubitably saved by every recipient for posterity's sake (if they weren't sold for a great deal of money on eBay!). It takes someone of taste to realize how much words of support and encouragement mean to those on the receiving end.

While she was making First Lady visits to the capitals of Europe and South America, her evening hairstyle was upswept with a bun on top—in the fantastic *brioche* style designed for her by Alexandre de Paris. The day after the photos appeared in the French press, French women went to their hairdressers to have that *brioche* hairstyle copied. The week following that, after the American press was thoroughly saturated with pictures of the Kennedy visit to France, American women began attempting the same look at their hair salons. There were a great number of women in the U.S. in the early 1960s telling their hairdressers, "You know, everyone tells me I look exactly like Jacqueline Kennedy, so I want my hair to be set like hers, too."

Jackie had an athletic build, with broad shoulders, well-toned arms, and a trim waist that defied anything not to fit properly. Unlike Clare Luce, she had the patience to stand for as many fittings as it took. Fashion was a priority in her life. Her practiced eye flagged any infinitesimal error in her designer clothes, from a button placed slightly off on the side panel of a skirt to a shoulder pad a couple of centimeters narrower than the opposite one.

New York designer and man-about-town Oleg Cassini would come to the White House in secret with his fitters to bring the clothes the First Lady had asked him to copy from the French designers. Fitters from the shop Chez Ninon in New York also had to be smuggled into the White House because the president certainly did not want my Social Office to be known as "the fashion mafia," which is exactly what one columnist called us.

Jackie moved like a ballet dancer in her clothes, always erect, agile, and totally flexible. Clare Luce would move with a hint of awkwardness and stiffness, as though she was uncomfortable in her beautiful clothes. Both women knew when the spotlight was on them, so when entering a crowd, they would walk straight ahead toward their destinations, smiling, heads up, backs straight, proud peacocks who appeared to be thinking deep and important thoughts, when in fact they were just trying to avoid being stopped for conversation by fans or people who pretended to know them personally.

Every Christmas, Jackie gave a gift to everyone who worked for the White House in some capacity (that meant well over two thousand people, including the ushers' office staff, secret service, security forces, kitchen and pastry chef staffs, code room staff, florist's shop, medical assistance, *Air Force One* pilots and chopper pilots, butlers, gardeners and maids, electronic gurus, plumbers, and others). Her gift was always very special—something framable, large, and impressive. There were watercolors of various White House public rooms that had been restored and refurbished by her White House Fine Arts Committee. One year it was a matted photograph of Caroline and John being driven by Mrs. Kennedy in a horse-drawn antique sleigh over the snow-covered White House grounds. It was always magical. Every employee of the White House would receive one, plus friends and staff from all the parts of their complex life—including the people who managed their various houses in Virginia, Hyannisport, and the winter retreat shared by the Kennedy family in Palm Beach. Each of these historic paintings or photographs was cosigned by the president and Mrs. Kennedy, with a charming holiday message. Imagine what the contents of that large, flat envelope meant to the people who received it in the December mail! The First Lady did not assign this task to one of the minions in the White House. She spent many days developing the gift herself and deciding how it was to be matted or framed, and how it was to be wrapped in special White House seal paper with gold ribbons.

She had been trained in those manners by her mother, Janet Bouvier (later Auchincloss). She did not simply learn them after Jack Kennedy won the presidential election. After state dinners in the White House, she would congratulate the chef and the staff in the kitchen for doing a superb job, which they always did. She would always remember to thank the head butler, who would pass on her remarks to all of the serving staff and the extras who had been called in to help with the dinner. Their broad smiles were proof of how much they treasured praise from the First Lady. From the time she was a young girl, she had been trained to go into the kitchen after a special dinner involving guests, in order to congratulate those responsible for the meal. The power of just a few words of thanks or praise is immeasurable.

Jackie cared about fashion, yes. In fact, she cared

very much about it. She received advance copies of all the top fashion magazines from France, Italy, and Great Britain, as well as the United States. Friends would go to survey the Paris couture collections and write to her about what was new and exciting. Designers would fly down from New York with huge assortments of clothes to show her. The bickering among the designers trying to dress La Jacqueline created too much press interest, too much oh là là Parisian couture fluff for the president and his tough politicians to swallow in the West Wing. The president felt that all this emphasis on clothes from France and Italy was harmful to the fashion industry in America and to his image. (Let us admit that the fashion trade publications reminded him of this weekly, and they blamed JFK for his having single-handedly destroyed the custom of men wearing hats.) Even worse, everyone wanted to gift Jackie with imported designer creations, which raised the hackles of the Internal Revenue Service, suspicious that the First Lady was not paying the proper duties on these imports. We counterattacked with proof that Mrs. Kennedy was a symbol of America the Beautiful and was working at her unsalaried job all the time, which required a wardrobe far beyond the

Sears and JCPenney seasonal offerings. I remember a U.S. customs agent arguing with me on this matter. "You didn't see Mrs. Truman and Mrs. Eisenhower buying all these fancy duds and skipping the import duties, did you?" he asked very unkindly. I dispatched one of my assistants to the press files, and she brought back to show the customs agent some photos of Bess (one of America's favorite First Ladies, I might add) and also of Mamie in their official regalia when they were First Ladies, and a couple of photos of Jackie in her designer official regalia. The problem was solved when Oleg Cassini was put in charge of her wardrobe. All European designers for the First Lady were temporarily banished, that is, in the eyes of the public. (Balenciaga, Dior, and Givenchy gowns still secretly made their way into the family quarters to be considered and perhaps purchased or at least copied.)

I remember Jackie from the time we were teenagers in Washington. I was three years older, but we often had lunch in the now defunct restaurant La Salle du Bois and went to many of the same parties. She would put on a tiny scarf with her pullover and wool skirt, and it would look as though it was a custom-made original outfit. I was among her female

friends who would go home and then try to twist my
scarf and make it look chic and stay put, as hers did. I
failed totally. She had a certain magic with all her
accessories—belts, gloves, earrings, whatever. She
always looked perfect, and perfectly balanced. She
would take off one or two things before going out
the door—perhaps an extra bracelet or the pearl
double-strand necklace, or perhaps the belt. Her eye
told her what everyone knew but few of us knew
how to demonstrate: "Less is more."

Of course, when her husband, Senator John
Kennedy, won the presidential election, her every
move was watched and photographed by what
seemed to her "a bunch of termites that keep coming
out of the woodwork." She became America's prized
princess, and everything she touched, wore, went to
see, ate, and used became immediately what every
other woman around the world wanted to emulate.

Jackie's simplicity of dress was the most important ingredient of her style. When it was announced
that the shah of Iran and his beautiful young wife,
the Empress Farah Diba, were coming to Washington on a state visit, everyone in the fashion world
was in a state of excitement not seen since Marie
Antoinette had her dressmakers prepare the queen's
new winter wardrobe. Farah Diba was dressed only

by the top French designers. It was announced she was bringing with her the crown jewels of Iran, a group of emeralds and diamonds of such magnificence, no one in the twentieth century could even comprehend them.

The jewelers in America rushed in with offers to lend the First Lady jewels to compete with Farah Diba's, but on the big night of the state dinner, Jackie appeared in a simple white and pale pink silk shantung sleeveless dress. Her jewelry consisted of a diamond pin in her upswept brioche hairdo (the hair designed by Alexandre de Paris, of course) and a touch of almost unseen glitter at the waist. Farah Diba appeared in a billowing ball gown of glittering gold (even the fabric had been specially woven for the House of Dior). Tall and majestic-looking, she could bear the weight of the diamonds and emeralds, but Jackie won that night hands down. The simplicity and charm of her dress and hair kept the crowd spellbound. She knew she couldn't compete in the jewelry contest because of the smashing glitter from Iran's treasury, so she went in the opposite direction—and it worked.

Jackie had a powerful influence on young girls, who considered her a combination of a Barbie doll and a magical queen. Influenced by Jackie's perfect posture, young women began to stand up straighter. The First Lady's good taste affected not only the mothers in America, but their daughters as well.

Her entertaining skills and her management of the beautifully restored interiors for the White House are covered in another part of this book, but there is no question that Jacqueline Bouvier Kennedy, later Onassis, had a profound influence on the world. Luckily, she had a sense of humor about it and would brush it off when people rhapsodized about her as if she had a certain magical power— except, of course, she knew perfectly well she did have it!

"The Best-Dressed Suit"

There used to be a handful of women in the world who were astonishingly and beautifully dressed at all times, whether they were shopping, going to the opera, attending a funeral, or catching a movie with a friend. We knew about their wardrobes because of the power of the late Eleanor Lambert's "Best Dressed List," which was heavily promoted by the fashion industry. She formulated it in 1940, it grew to be a powerful publicity vehicle for designers and manufacturers, and it was often said that "most women would kill to be on it." There was an American list and a European one. (Any Asian or South American women who were put on the list bought their clothes in Paris, so the European list encompassed every country other than the United States.) The American list over the years has included Jacqueline Kennedy and her sister, Lee Radziwill, designer Carolina Herrera, Grace Kelly, Nancy Reagan, Bianca Jagger, and movie stars like Nicole Kidman and Angelina Jolie. The European list has included Princess Diana; Principessa Luciana Pignatelli; Contessa Letizia Pecci-Blunt; Wallis, the Duchess of Windsor; Baroness de Rothschild; the Maharani of Jaipur; Princess Paola of Belgium; Vicomtesse Jacqueline de Ribes; and the American sisters-in-law Vivi Crespi and Gloria Crespi, who married Italian counts. The Best Dressed List was a commercial ploy to entice women into buying more clothes, but it achieved a much more affirmative goal. Women copied the fashions of the ladies on the list and consequently learned a great deal about how to dress, as well as how to transform the philosophy behind these expensive clothes into their own affordable wardrobes.

I kept track of these zippy, ultra-attractive clotheshorses in the last century during my diplomatic career abroad because the first priority on their traveling social schedules was to be received by the American ambassador when they were in Paris, Rome, or London. Some of them felt that just because they were on the Best Dressed List, they deserved special treatment. An invitation to a mere embassy cocktail party was demeaning to them. They felt they deserved the honor of a formal dinner.

Fashion changes every decade or so, but the standards today are very different from the days of yore. The youth revolution and the decline in standards has upended the formerly strict rules of modesty and appropriateness in dress. One sees blue jeans on guests and official visitors to the White House. One sees shorts worn with men's shirts at the opera. The royal reverence that Eleanor Lambert's list used to elicit is gone. Published reports on the price of the wedding dress worn by movie mogul Aaron Spelling's daughter is what the public wants to hear.

Women of substance, such as Clare Boothe Luce, pretended to ridicule the Best Dressed List, but Luce was in a celebratory mood for at least a week after her name was added to it in the 1950s. There used to be a continuous dribble (unlike today, when it's never a dribble, but a torrent) of photos taken of fashionable women at large society events and charitable fund-raisers. When a couple of women broke society's un-published rules in the 1940s and posed for a paid advertisement for a product (Pond's cold cream, for one), it had enough shock value to make them a sub-ject for criticism for a long time. The Old Guard sniffed mightily, even if one of its gossip victims claimed she had posed for the ad "only to give the money to charity."

Until the 1950s, real society held that one's name could properly be mentioned in the press only at birth or at death, or for a debut and a wedding in-between. By the 1930s, there were posed photos of prominent, beautiful women, taken by famous pho-tographers (Horst and Cecil Beaton, for example) for magazines like *Vogue, Vanity Fair, Harper's Bazaar,* and *Town & Country.* A woman of society, dressed in jodhpurs, a perfectly fitted tweed jacket, a black velvet riding hat, gloves, and polished boots of the finest leather, was considered a bona fide celebrity as she was photographed on her horse or in a fabulous ball gown, gracefully seated on an antique sofa in her library, perhaps holding an elongated, diamond-studded ebony cigarette holder between her second and third fingers. Or she might be photographed at work in her estate gardens, wearing a pretty sundress and espadrilles, and a giant straw hat to protect her perfect white skin. One always suspected that there were at least two estate gardeners hiding behind the trees so as not to appear in the photos shot by legendary photographer Slim Aarons for a feature in *Look* magazine.

Ladies were often photographed in their ancestral mansions on Long Island or Lake Forest or Atlanta, on the terraces of their vacation homes in Newport, Santa Barbara, or Jamaica, or sitting on the stern of their yachts moored in Palm Beach or Acapulco. Today's woman tends to be photographed in her oversized modern kitchen, reviewing plans with a chef or caterer for a lavish dinner party, held perhaps to bolster her corporate husband's position with his company or to launch a major fund-raiser for charity, which would definitely heighten her social visibility. Her kitchen would have been designed by a godlike designer of kitchens, of course. To have him even consult on such an area in her house would add perhaps another twenty-five thousand dollars to the cost of construction.

But in days of yore, such a woman would never have been found near her kitchen. Her accomplished cook, butler, and maids would have seen to all the meal preparations. Today, everyone is expected to be a "foodie" and to have gourmet culinary expertise, which is often a joke to those who know the hosters well, particularly if she is on an eternal diet.

The wives of Thoroughbred racehorse owners used to attract the society press during racing season at Saratoga, Belmont, Newport, and, of course, the unequaled Kentucky Derby in Lexington. The "Southern and the lockjawed society broads" is how one irreverent sports reporter described these women at the track. They inevitably appeared in enormous hats decorated with flowers, and in gloves, of course. It was America's attempt at having our own Ascot. The same sports reporter made fun of the ladies' accents—some dripping with Southern molasses, others proclaiming Long Island origins. "Locust Valley Lockjaw" speech could be described as the sounds of someone speaking through the nose and teeth without ever moving the jaw.

Except for major events like the Kentucky Derby the social *aficionadas* of the sport of racing are much less visible in today's press. And no one seems to give extravagant parties anymore like Mary Lou Whitney's stellar ones at Saratoga. The Ladies of Racing, like the Ladies of the Opera, Ballet, and Concerts, have been replaced in the press by entertainment magnets who show more skin than fashion—notables like Jennifer Lopez, Halle Berry, Paris Hilton, and Britney Spears.

And, of course, the fashion press has always covered the debutante balls all over the country. Today, there is much less emphasis on them as pure social events, and more emphasis on the considerable amounts of money these cotillions can raise for charity. I have always looked at the photographs in the magazines of the young debs with great interest. They tell the history of young women in America who, instead of just partying, are now working, becoming lawyers and doctors, getting their master's degrees, and still managing to care very much about their white debutante dresses. Hooray for them, but perhaps there are some notes of caution to be given about taste. I saw one recent debutante in a lavish white designer gown, proudly showing off the genuine tattoos of pink roses on her bare shoulders. She would benefit by knowing the stories of America's doyennes of taste.

Notable Women of Taste

The most important aspect of the following women of yesteryear, quite apart from their fashion influence on American women, was that they were very nice people!

C. Z. Guest

One of the famous Cochran sisters of Boston, C. Z. Guest was the perfect prototype of a fragile, pale porcelain beauty. Enviably slim, and with a head of always perfect blond hair, she wore pastel satin Mainbocher evening sheaths that made her look, as one society columnist described it, like "an exquisite fresh water pearl." Together with her husband, millionaire sportsman and big-game hunter Winston Guest, she was extremely busy, preoccupied with the gardens of her husband's family estate, Westbury Gardens, on Long Island, which were open to the public. Her friends, knowing how much time she had to spend at the hairdressers and spas to keep looking that way, were amazed to see her getting down in the dirt to tend to her flowers and plants, and to experiment in crossbreeding and in growing exotic species. Tourists arrived by the busload to tour the Guests' Westbury

Gardens, and before her friends could believe it, C. Z. had gone into the gardening business herself, becoming a successful syndicated newspaper columnist on the subject. Every time she and I crossed paths, she would quiz me on my latest experiences in the corporate world. At the turn of the twenty-first century, after years of serving as a familiar, beautiful face in New York's smartest nightclubs, she began to proudly refer to herself as "a business executive."

As one of her North Shore friends said, "No one can do with a bouquet of a thousand flowers what C. Z. can do with one geranium in her hand."

Babe Paley

One of the famous Cushing sisters, Babe Paley was one of the most celebrated beauties of the twentieth century. Blessed with striking dark eyes, thick black hair, and creamy white skin, she was a showstopper wherever she went. Upon entering a room, she was used to having people stop talking in order to stare at her without interruption. Her last marriage, to William Paley, the head of CBS, was an unhappy one from which she suffered physically and emotionally. But she always looked like three billion, not a million. Those sensational clothes—and those Schlumberger and Verdura jewels!

Babe Paley was one of the great hostesses who came into Tiffany's when I was head of public relations there. She had been invited to design a table setting as part of a hostess exhibition on the second and third floors of the store. She asked if she could create a breakfast setting as her contribution, which, of course, was fine with the store, but we all thought it was a rather humble request—until we realized it was an inside joke. She brought from her bedroom at home a spacious flowered chaise longue, and next to it she set up a small round Billy Baldwin–designed table, with a tray containing a small sterling coffeepot, a sugar bowl and creamer, a delicate porcelain cup and saucer and silver spoon, plus a lovely little crystal glass for orange juice. There was a pale green cashmere throw on the chaise, plus a copy of a wildly popular novel by her great friend Truman Capote, left lying open, with her spectacles resting upon it. When we saw that the book was entitled *Breakfast at Tiffany's,* we caught on to her joke. Babe and Truman came into the store to choose the Tiffany china and crystal for her breakfast setup, giggling with delight at their clever idea as they completed her setting. (This was in the period when they were the closest of friends, but unfortunately, they later had a much publicized falling-out and never spoke to one another again.)

I was not alone in feeling like an ugly duckling in Babe's presence, but people will always remember her for her gracious smile and warm, kind heart. I think Babe would be happy to know that she was remembered for that instead of the fact that she made thousands of women jealous of her beauty, wardrobe, and fortune.

Pauline Potter

Pauline Potter had a terrible childhood. She grew up unloved, impoverished, and shunted from place to place, which may very well be the reason for her strength and willpower to accomplish her goals. She rose above all the difficulties because of her enormous zest, style, and intellectual bent.

She ultimately became famous for her food, flowers, and imaginative entertaining. No detail was ever left to chance. She filled the empty spaces in her house with vases of white lilacs and lilies. Weekend guests found an attractive woven basket on the table in their room, filled with notepaper, letter paper, airmail paper, stamps, postcards, and pens. Another little tray lay alongside it, featuring a bottle of mineral water, a stemmed crystal goblet, an assortment of small crustless cucumber and watercress sandwiches, an empty plate, fresh fruit in a basket, a fork and fruit knife, and some crisp cookies on a little saucer, in case a moment of hunger were to interfere with her guests' sleep.

Pauline was famous for her table settings, which evolved from her habit of setting up before a party meal a miniature "tablescape," like a miniature dress rehearsal showing the elements of her decorating theme for that particular meal, whether it was a sampling of unusual leaves and moss from her garden, an unusual fabric used for her napkins, or unexpected bibelots she would place in various spots on the table.

While hunting in France one time she appeared in thigh-high suede Three Musketeers–like boots, setting off an immediate fad back in America. Unfortunately, many of the women who copied her were short or had chubby legs. Those who realized this exotic fashion was not appropriate for them because their legs weren't like the Baroness de Rothschild's were exercising their good taste!

Pauline began perfecting her hostess abilities with small dinner parties for six or eight in her two-room apartment in Baltimore and later in New York. No one knew how she could do it in such a small space. As she became a successful fashion magazine editor, she also became a successful dress designer. She exuded an air of originality in everything on her and around her. I remember her from my Paris days, talking spiritedly on subjects of intellectual or cultural interest. Her voice was so beautiful that people strained to hear every word. She may have been decidedly unbeautiful, but she turned this deficit into a plus as she stretched even taller, wore stunning clothes, and always stood out from the crowd.

After an unhappy first marriage, she married the Baron Philippe de Rothschild, who had taken over the family wine business. It had closed down during the war, but he built it up again into the thriving Mouton Rothschild vintage wines. It became one of the greatest Bordeaux vineyards in the world.

Pauline helped her husband with the new designs for the labels on the wine bottles. There was a new series, for example, designed by famous artists of the day—Picasso, Cocteau, and Salvador Dalí. People began to save their empty bottles because of the labels, and a few even stooped to decanting lesser wines for their dinner parties into empty Rothschild bottles bearing a great artist's label.

Pauline was one of Evangeline Bruce's good friends, and one night she appeared at an embassy reception in a simple black dress, off-the-shoulder. When she entered the salon, conversation momentarily ceased. A journalist friend of mine, who knew I'd be seeing the "célèbre Baronesse de Rothschild" at the reception, called me the next day for a description of her attire.

"She wore a body-slimming, unadorned black dress with a big diamond clip in the lower left corner of her décolletage, and high-heeled black satin pumps," I answered.

"And?" questioned my impatient friend.

"And nothing," I replied. Just that. The stunning black dress with a single accent—a large, asymmetrical diamond brooch—and dark satiny eyeshadow framing her oversized eyes. It was enough. She held the entire room captive with her intelligent conversation until she left the embassy residence.

Audrey Hepburn

Audrey Hepburn has been called a nymph, an enchantress, an eternal schoolgirl, the most sophisticated of seductive women, and the most enthusiastic, mature ingenue in the business. She was all of those, but much more.

Hepburn burst into America's consciousness as a movie actress in the heady postwar period of the 1950s and '60s, becoming a siren in the '70s. She made the sleeveless sheath and the Givenchy square-shouldered look and unusual neckline the fashion that everyone wanted to copy (and many couture designers actually did). Although she was an unknown when her movie *Roman Holiday* appeared in theaters, she single-handedly pushed Rome into the number-one travel destination in the Western world. She woke up the world to the Vespa motorscooter when she and Gregory Peck traveled around Rome, Audrey perched daintily on the rear, clutching Gregory Peck with her arms around his waist. So innocent-looking and so sexy!

Her biggest fans were the men who played opposite her, including Cary Grant. In one scene she cried on Cary Grant's well-tailored shoulder and ad-libbed an apology for getting his jacket all wet. His ad-lib comeback was perfect: don't worry, he told her, "the suit is drip-dry." Together they had bested the scriptwriters!

Her basic fashion creed was very similar to Jacqueline Kennedy's, with a stress on totally simple, sleeveless sheaths, worn with pearls at the neck. Women all over the world struggled to copy her constantly changing short haircuts, to make up their faces like hers, and to wear tight-fitting black pants like hers, paired with ballet flats. She often tied a scarf around her head, but the hats in her films, large and small, were important to Hepburn's signature look. In the

1961 film made of Truman Capote's novel *Breakfast at Tiffany's*, she wore a large floppy mink hat with her bright orange Givenchy-designed wool coat. Both the color orange and the floppy mink hat became stars in retail stores that year. Her pillbox hats were consciously or unconsciously copied by Jackie Kennedy, even for the president's Inauguration Day. Audrey's giant black sunglasses from the same film kept the sunglass manufacturers in the black for many years, and that fad continues even today.

Mothers bought records of Audrey's speaking voice and played them endlessly to their daughters, hoping they could somehow absorb the tonality and the charming accent of the actress. I actually saw a pregnant woman in Chicago's Lincoln Park holding a tape cassette of Audrey's voice against her stomach in the hopes that the tonality and rhythm of that charming voice would somehow pass through to her unborn child!

When *Breakfast at Tiffany's* was made, the filming took several days inside and outside the store. On the set is where the true character of important stars emerges. Audrey Hepburn charmed everyone, from the night watchman and the timekeeper at the side entrance to the elevator operators and the salesclerks. She shook hands with everyone she saw, flashed those dark brown eyes wide open with her smile, and said to everyone, "Oh, I'm so glad to meet you!" just as though she meant it.

Carmel Snow

The late and very great editor in chief of *Harper's Bazaar* in its heyday, Carmel Snow, once gave me some very good advice. It was in New York in 1956, when I was just beginning my Tiffany's job. (I knew her daughters, Bridget and "little Carmel," which is how I got up the courage to invite her to lunch and ask for some instant advice.) I was lamenting my lack of real knowledge of the fashion industry, and the fact that since I had been in Europe at the American embassy in the preceding years, I had lost contact with Seventh Avenue. "I don't know who the real tastemakers are in this country," I complained.

"I'm not going to give you a bunch of names," Carmel said. "Visit all the top showrooms, look at who's come to see the collection and how they're dressed, and if you see someone you feel is unusually well put together when you're out at lunch or even shopping, find out who it is. Knowing who these women are will serve you well." She made me do all the work, which is just what a wise teacher does.

Snow was a woman of few words, but she told me in plain language that to learn the business and recognize its real leaders, "you have to use your eyes." Those eyes again. Everything stems from the eyes, it seems, when developing a sense of taste. "Memorize details of something that looks good," she commanded, "but be sure to know how to look at it in the first place, so that you zero in only on the important details. Not every detail is worthy of attention."

I asked her for career advice, and she gave it. I was stepping into a job about which I knew nothing—head of public relations for Tiffany's. "Don't waste people's time," she said sternly. "Go and observe closely in a place where you'll see the workings of publicity and public relations up close. I'll ask Elizabeth Penrose Hawkins, the woman's editor of *The New York Times,* to let you sit by her desk, in silence, for one whole day. Everyone sends her their products, releases, and photographs, hoping *The Times* will pick up the story and print it. Most of it is garbage. Just watch how she sorts it out and separates the impossible releases from the possible ones, and even from the very few interesting ones. Watch how her eye works."

I will never forget Carmel Snow for that. I learned

enough in one day about how to handle my job for Tiffany, sitting by Mrs. Hawkins, to substitute for three years in journalism school.

Diana Vreeland

A figure that stands out in deep relief in the history of America's taste is Diana Vreeland. She was not a beautiful woman. She was simply the most dramatic, theatrical, startling center of fashion in her era. She made Auntie Mame look pallid. She was married to a very handsome man, Reed Vreeland, who unfortunately was not a moneymaker. She had to work and fight hard to keep Reed and their two equally handsome sons afloat. She was a firecracker, with an energy that mowed down anyone who was in her path.

She became known for her uncanny ability to predict fashion trends when she was working at *Harper's Bazaar*. Then, in 1962, she stepped into fashion's biggest job and became editor in chief of *Vogue*. Before trying to change the fashion look in the United States, she decided to give herself a makeover. She gave up her controversial habit of wearing her hair in a snood with a ribbon bow on top, and bobbed her black hair to the chin, then smoothed it back behind her ears. No one else had worn her hair that way, but suddenly many began to try. She had big ears, and she highlighted them with rouge, rather than try to make them appear smaller. She always wore armfuls of avant-garde bangles—ivory, ebony, and gold jewelry that made noise when she moved. She brandished a cigarette holder, too, like the baton of a symphony conductor.

Diana Vreeland knew before anyone else what was coming into fashion. Yet she also knew when to stop, pull in, simplify. She advised Jackie during the White House years, giving her stylistic tips that were incredibly important—wearing a pillbox hat to match her wool coat on Inauguration Day and keeping her hands warm in a mink muff. She led *Vogue* through the youth rebellion of the 1970s and made readers understand what all this meant to fashion. She initiated the first "lifestyle" articles on celebrities and society figures in the magazine, going into their homes and photographing their parties and their life of sports and hobbies. She turned young society girls like Penelope Tree and Loulou de la Falaise into famous models, and she made unusual faces and bodies—like those of Lauren Hutton and Verushka—the toast of the country. She got her readers into sports and exercise, weight-reduction programs, hair treatments, and plastic surgery. She was a pioneer in the art of makeovers.

She thought that the cardinal sin was to be boring, which she never was. She was one of the first to paint her living room a dark red lacquer. When she did a table setting at one of Tiffany's famous designer table-setting shows, she brought in what seemed like a ton of sand (it was all over Tiffany's china floor for weeks). She had a tent constructed with four giant freestanding gold-plated palm trees to serve as the tent supports. Then she set a dinner on an oriental rug spread on the sand, just as an important princely Arab sheik would do it, using Tiffany's vermeil (golden) plates and any manner of exotic containers for the food. Diana called it "Dinner with the sheik in the desert." A woman from Brooklyn, touring all of the table settings in the exhibition with a friend, announced loudly her opinion of the Vreeland setting: "Do you think this woman is a nut? I mean, who would live like this? Who would eat on the sand? And those gold palm trees? It's just crazy." Just then an imperious voice came out of nowhere. Diana had happened to be there and had overheard the complaint. "Who would live like this?" she asked sarcastically. "Just anyone who's anyone would live like this!" Her voice was booming. She wore leopard-print pants and slippers, a black turtleneck, and her ever present jewelry. She scared the two ladies from Brooklyn to such an extent that they fled to the elevators, leaving all of us convulsed in laughter.

When Jackie Kennedy became First Lady, the first person she wrote to before moving into the White House was Diana Vreeland, begging for her help on the sensitive issue of her own First Lady fashion problems. Diana helped her work with both French and American designers, saying nothing to the press and helping smooth over the problems we faced with schedules, credits, and press leaks.

She was always quotable, famous for statements such as "Shocking pink is the navy blue of India." She hated narcissism and yet approved of vanity, but her most famous phrase in my opinion was "What sells is hope." I borrowed it from her all through my professional life.

I will always remember her fondly for something she did for me when I was working as Tiffany's first female executive and setting up their first department of publicity. Walter Hoving, the head of the company, had put my office in a drafty back corridor above the trade entrance. Diana came to see me on a properly arranged appointment concerning some exotic idea she had for photographing Jean Schlumberger's jewelry for *Vogue* in a Dalí-esque setting. The only way she could get to me was by coming through the trade entrance in back of the store. When she stepped off the trade elevator, jammed with carts piled high with boxes, she literally had to fall into my office the minute the doors opened. She looked at my miserable office setup, with the elevator opening and closing on us constantly, and she became enraged. Without saying a word to me, she stormed back downstairs, went through the trade entrance and then up onto the fifth floor on the Fifth Avenue side, into the executive offices. She walked right in on Mr. Hoving without announcing herself and, from all reports, spoke loudly and angrily at this male chauvinist who was treating me in such a terrible fashion. She kept saying, "Walter, it's a scandal! A scandal!" To have La Vreeland screaming at him unsettled Walter Hoving no end. Two days later, my department was in a striking wood-paneled office on the Fifth Avenue side of the executive floor. She had fought an important battle for me, and that is something one does not forget.

Diana's last "job" as someone who had to work to

support herself was a prestigious one: special consultant to the Metropolitan Museum of Art's Costume
Institute. Her exhibits were big hits with the public,
even if her scholarship was questioned in some art
circles. It didn't really matter. The public came and
loved what it saw. She bowed out of the working
world in 1986 and died in 1989, but not before she
had influenced the taste of hundreds of thousands of
women in her time. She added excitement and piz-
zazz to that taste, like a perfectly seasoned dish.

Nan Kempner

I remember the late Nan Kempner (Mrs. Thomas),
who loved clothes and the publicity she attracted
wearing them. She was tall, slim, and dressed with
such bravado that men and women were awestruck
when she made her dramatic entrance to a party.
She could have been wearing an old tablecloth, but
on her, it looked chic. She was slavishly copied, but
since she had such great style, no one quite got
there. They couldn't copy her energized way of
moving and her constant laughter and sparkling
eyes, all of which added to the impression created
by her clothes. Like Katharine Hepburn and Marlene Dietrich, she was at her very best in meticu-
lously cut trousers, with a silk shirt with cuff links,

or a cashmere sweater, or a combination of both. *Insouciance,* the French call it.

Margaret, the Duchess of Argyll

When good taste is on parade, anyone in the vicinity seems to sense it. I'll never forget the "royal walk-through" made by the Duchess of Argyll on a visit to New York. This wasn't Buckingham Palace in London or even a castle in Scotland. She made this journey through the center aisle of Bloomingdale's mammoth department store, from the entrance on Lexington Avenue through to the other end on Third Avenue. It was in early October, a sunny but cool day, and the store was packed with shoppers who had long since finished their back-to-school buying for the children. They were into themselves, not their kids.

Margaret was dressed from head to toe in cream and cocoa brown colors, from her high-heeled suede pumps and handbag to the sheer veil that crossed her forehead and tied behind, holding her dark auburn hair in a perfectly shaped coiffure. Even her eyeshadow and lipstick matched. Now this was over sixty years ago, but not only can I see her clearly now, but so could every New Yorker—customer or salesperson—in the store at that time. It was as though the biblical waters were parting again as people stepped to the side to get a better look at her. As she began her walk, the busy hum of department store chatter ceased. There was an electricity in the air, so everyone turned to see from which direction it came. With a warm smile (aimed at no one in particular), but fully, happily aware that all the stares were in her direction, she walked slowly through the now empty center aisle. She glanced quickly at the merchandise left and right, stopping when she saw something that particularly interested her. Chunky gold, jeweled bracelet charms escaped from under the top of her kid gloves. With her head erect, her posture perfect, this was a perfectly stunning woman who knew it and who was obviously determined to keep her image intact. The questions "Who is *that*? Who is she?" were whispered throughout the store in tones of near reverence.

"That's the Duchess of Argyll from Scotland," I told the clerk hovering over the newly arrived silk umbrellas from Italy.

"You know her?" The clerk looked stunned.

"I've met her a couple of times."

"Well, then, go up to her! Say hello to her!"

"No, I don't think so," I said, returning my scrutiny to the umbrellas.

She would not let it go. "Why not? Why aren't you going to speak to her?" Her disappointment was acute.

"I'm not a friend. Meeting someone does not constitute a relationship. Anyway, I wouldn't want to disturb her on her mission to this store."

"Well, *I* certainly would go up to her," the clerk replied, "for an autograph, and then I'd tell her I'd never seen anyone so gloriously dressed, and I would never ever forget her auburn hair and veil, and pumps and all. She looks like a magnificent butterscotch sundae!"

I was sorry I didn't encourage the clerk to go speak to the duchess herself. She would have given Margaret of Argyll such a big dose of morale-raising, but then again the clerk might have been fired by Bloomie's for having done so. One does not unnecessarily bother "the Royals."

Grace Kelly, Alias Her Serene Highness
The three best-looking wives of heads of state in the second half of the twentieth century were known for their fashion expertise as well as their beauty. (Princess Diana would have made this a quartet, except for her youthfulness and the fact that her husband was not yet head of his country.) The three

were Jackie Kennedy, Empress Farah Diba of Iran, and Princess Grace of Monaco. Grace was dressed by the top fashion designers in the movie industry, then by leading French designers when she stepped into the role of wife of Prince Rainier of Monaco. Jackie was dressed by American designer Oleg Cassini and Paris designer Valentino. The empress was French couture all the way. The fashion sense of the women was as important to their success with the press and the populace as their husbands' political moves were.

Grace and Jack Kennedy reportedly had a fling before either was married, so when it came time for the official visit of Their Serene Highnesses to Washington, the visit was mysteriously downgraded from a grand gala evening state dinner to a lunch for twenty or so. Jackie was not about to have Princess Grace, shining with her blond beauty and wearing a fantastic ball gown, sweeping around the White House at a state dinner by candlelight. Nothing was less glamorous than a luncheon at noon. Hollywood was disappointed, to say nothing of how Princess Grace felt, but that is the way life goes.

Although Prince Rainier was his usual smiling, proper self at lunch in the White House, his wife openly flirted by casting large goo-goo eyes at the president. This comical situation was captured by a

White House photographer and became one of the most celebrated candid photos of any state function.

Grace disappointed us that day from a fashion point of view. She wore a suit by her favorite American designer, but the famous blond hair was totally hidden under a tall white Lilly Daché turban. The hat was encrusted (one White House wag said it was "infested") with little white blossoms all over. Her turban ended up looking exactly like a blossom-studded bathing cap belonging to swim star Esther Williams.

There were so many more doyennes of taste in those days of yore, including Jessica Daves, editor in chief of *Vogue* for many years, Babs Simpson, Bettina Ballard, and a host of other really great women who taught everyone how to dress, entertain, and behave in their beautiful clothes, and who, in fact, shaped more than the taste of the American woman.

*I*f you watch women of taste being questioned by the press about what they are wearing, they are polite but do not necessarily share the desired information. "Who made your suit? Are those Ferragamo pumps? Is that a Ralph Lauren raincoat?" Some of these women act as though they didn't hear the question.

They are very different from the stars and would-be stars on Hollywood's red carpet who depend on the amount of publicity they can attract, and who would credit the designer of their underwear if they could. It's a life of paybacks to the people in the industry who lend or give them free clothes. The model on the fashion magazine cover wearing an upside-down frilly lampshade on her head, with matching frills atop her laced-up black dominatrix boots, or wearing a Greek mini toga made of a see-through plasticlike material, with a crown of laurel leaves on her head, may be able to carry it off—but only because she is drop-dead beautiful, has yards of hair attachments streaming all over like Aphrodite rising from the sea, and is posed on a photographer's set with dreamy clouds and trick lighting flashing like thunder and lightning around her. The average woman isn't usually immersed in thunder and lightning when she appears in public. Nor would she wear what looks like a chorus girl's lacy corset atop a heavy Irish tweed skirt trimmed on the bottom with two rolls of pastel organdy trim, and laced leather boots with five-inch heels to finish it off. An attractive woman who tries to copy that model's total look might resemble someone who has gone bonkers, rather than a woman of great style.

I have always noticed that women in the public eye who have taste have fewer things in their closets than the wanna-bes striving to get on the Best Dressed List. They're not afraid to wear their clothes time and time again. A really good suit, for example, can be looked upon as new if it is worn with a different blouse or shell, or accessorized with an interesting scarf, or worn with a jewel or an artificial flower on the lapel. It's much more important—and less expensive—to dress with good taste than to feel compelled to sashay around in the newest fashion fad for the short season that is being promoted by fashion editors and the retail trade.

So much for being a slave to the fashion media. Before we make a major purchase, we should make love to a big mirror. We should stare at ourselves wearing it—front, back, and sideways. How do we look sitting down in it? If we perceive a trace of freakiness somewhere in our appearance, we can be confident that there is. Therefore, no sale!

Good Taste in Jewelry

If you stop to think of it, jewelry crosses many lines. It is certainly fashion. It is certainly art, based on designs by the greatest artists in the world. For centuries it has been used as barter, extortion, a spoil of war, and as a seductive female weapon. It has made some insurance companies rich. It has served as an economic standard for governments, as well as ransom, plunder, and a reason for making sophisticated thief films starring the James Bonds and the Cary Grants of this world.

Among the many great lessons I learned as Clare Luce's assistant was the knowledge that natural beauty combined with great jewelry conquers all. It didn't matter that her designer dress did not fit properly around the top of her neck but slid over to one side—no one looked at that. She would have the perfect jewel pinned to her waist on a wide satin sash—such as a large gold, pearl, and diamond brooch of a mythological winged horse with a ruby eye. Anyone talking to her would be immediately mesmerized by that jewel and never notice her neck.

In the evening in those Rome days, a ball gown was called for at 9 P.M. diplomatic dinners and other functions. Then she would be decked out with enough diamonds, emeralds, rubies, or sapphires to illuminate a dark alley. She was a blond beauty, with blue eyes that devastated any man looking into them. One night, when I was on my way to a black-tie dinner at the Palazzo Lovatelli dressed in a black satin gown, I remarked sadly to my boss how ugly and unfestive I felt, due to the large pimple on my nose.

"I'll fix that," she said. "Here, with this on top of your shoulder, no one will look at your nose." She attached a large diamond and turquoise brooch on the outside top edge of my shoulder, and I wore it proudly for the night. It worked. No one looked at my nose.

The late great designers in the jewelry field—Jean Schlumberger, Fulco Verdura, and David Webb—must be looking down from their heavenly perches absolutely aghast at what has happened to their *métier* in an era of loud costume jewelry. Designers Coco Chanel and Elsa Schiaparelli managed to saturate the fashion market with stunning real and fake jewelry after World War II, but never before has the world been so afloat with with copies, fakes, and thousands upon thousands of brilliants and beads, imitation stones and paste pearls sewn onto garments and underwear, attached to coiffures, worn on shoes and raincoats, or just serving as necklaces and bracelets covering acres of bare skin, including men's, and children's, too. The "bling" in today's jewelry is theatrical, blaring and glaring.

Some women look bling, blang, and blung with all the glitter hanging from them. The gold craftsmen of ancient Greece, Persia, Egypt, and Mesopotamia would be astonished to find all of the ornamentation, ersatz or real, worn by the earth's inhabitants of every economic class. In their day, only the exceedingly rich and the bravest of warriors had access to jewelry. It was always a rule of taste for a woman to highlight her major pieces of jewelry against a plain background. She would never wear it all at once. Today, by contrast, some women could be labeled walking Christmas trees, or, as one Palm Beach bachelor said, "a fireworks display with more fizzle and fazzle than authentic dazzle."

Other traditional rules, perhaps decreed just for the pleasure of breaking them, were:

- Diamonds should not be worn before 5 P.M.
- Real and costume jewelry should not be mixed.
- Gold and silver should not be mixed.
- Jewelry should be absolutely silent.
- It is bad taste to ask to "try on" a person's ring.
- It is incredibly bad taste to ask the owner of the ring how much it cost, or even worse, if it's a genuine stone or a fake.

- One's ring should always be kept sparkling clean, so that the owner will never need to make excuses for it when someone is praising it, protesting, "Oh, but it's so dirty! I must clean it." (One wonders why something so small is so difficult to keep clean.)

Women and Their Jewelry

Speaking of jewelry, a woman of taste does not wear a preponderance of rhinestone jewelry in the daytime—far too much bling. If she does, she might resemble a sparkling chandelier electrically lit but aimlessly shining in the noonday sun.

Marlene Dietrich once said, "Real jewelry looks divine, morning, noon, and night. Diamonds need sunshine every once in a while because it makes them grow better!" But a woman who wears diamonds should make certain to wear them discreetly in public and to be aware of safety at all times.

Unlike rhinestones, which glitter happily only after 6 P.M., diamonds (in a controlled amount) are appropriate all day. But regardless of the hour, to wear a diamond necklace, brooch, bracelets, ring, and earrings simultaneously is overkill, and a transgression against taste. (Let us hope that any over-diamonded lady has an excellent insurance policy!)

Men and Their Jewelry

Some men are so afraid of being called effeminate that they won't even use the term *jewelry* for what they do wear, including:

- A wristwatch.
- A belt buckle (silver, gold, or *vermeil*). A man with cultural ties to the West might wear a prize rodeo belt of hammered silver or gold, perhaps tastefully studded with turquoise. If he is a real Westerner, he would wear such a buckle only if he had performed in rodeos himself, or if the prize had been won by a male member of his family.
- A gold signet ring (engraved with the crest of a military academy or university of distinction, or engraved with the family crest). Very tacky: when a person has a gold ring made with a fake family crest; it is a sad attempt at showing the world one comes from an "old family."

- A tie clip or tie pin.
- Evening studs and cuff links (the smaller and the more low-key, the better). Traditionally popular are cuff links and matching studs in gold and pearl, all gold, or platinum with very small diamonds or other gemstones. I remember in my Tiffany days when the great designer Jean Schlumberger first introduced a set of small black hematite acorn cuff links, set in gold, with matching studs. They were tiny but completely beautiful and luminous, and they remained bestsellers for decades.
- Watches for men for black-tie evenings. Men can change their brown leather watchbands to stainless-steel watchbands for evening. An eighteen-karat gold watch on a gold bracelet or a platinum and diamond watch on a black suede wristband is subtle, beautiful, and, incidentally, very costly!
- Necklaces, often gold or sterling chains, or for the more affluent, specially designed pieces of precious metals, sometimes with a jeweler's talisman or dangling jeweled charm. These are popularly worn in the gay and Hispanic communities, and their acceptance is governed by each community's own strict laws of taste.

The Pearl Necklace

On the eve of my departure for graduate study in Europe, which I have always considered the true beginning of my life, my sweet father, in a moment of sentiment and sadness at seeing his "little girl go off to dangerous, wartorn Europe in 1946," decided to present me with our family's only really valuable jewelry—a very long ("opera length," it was called) string of natural, oriental pearls.

It was a rite of passage. I was now a mature woman, supposedly, and my father had been keeping the necklace for me. (It had been a payment from a woman to my father for legal services in lieu of money, a not uncommon event during the Great Depression of the '30s.)

My father's gift of the superbly long necklace of real pearls was all very "grande dame," so as a young woman, I doubted I would ever wear it. But it would have hurt my father's feelings not to have acted genuinely thrilled when he gave it to me.

Natural pearls came from oysters as an accident of nature. Since the days of ancient Persia these oysters were found in the murky waters of the Persian Gulf. They were brought up to the surface by young females specially trained in the precarious art of deep-sea diving. Many lost their lives in the pursuit of this profession, regardless of their unequaled lung capacity and aquatic strength. As a result of their labors in amassing collections of exquisite pearls in many shapes and colors, the royal families of Egypt, Persia, China, and Russia were able to own the most magnificent jewelry yet seen in the world. When the cultured-pearl industry began in Japan, it was the greatest news in the jewelry field since craftsmen were first trained to cut, polish, and set stones. By 1940 farm beds of oysters were growing an amazing new product in Japan. Some genius had discovered a way of growing pearls by injecting an irritant, such as a grain of sand, into a live oyster in its shell, which then caused it, under careful cultivation procedures, to grow pearl-like layers of skin outside the nucleus in a more or less round shape. These cultured pearls were never quite as beautiful and rare as the natural oriental ones, but it was often difficult to tell the difference between them with the naked eye.

In time, Kokichi Mikimoto and other smaller dealers in Japan grew the cultured-pearl business into a giant international industry. Tiffany finally broke down and carried them in 1956, having sold only oriental pearls until then because the cultured ones were considered artificial and not up to Tiffany's standards.

I had no idea of the real value of oriental pearls. All I knew was that I wanted to go with my American embassy colleague Mike Forrestal from Paris to Austria and Yugoslavia during an embassy leave. We finally, after great effort, received our precious visas. We would be the first Americans allowed to go as tourists into Tito's Yugoslavia since before World War II. It was dangerous and exciting. It was still a Communist country under a dictatorship. Mike and I figured out that our trip driving in his convertible from France into Yugoslavia and back to Paris would cost each of us about five hundred dollars (a princely sum in 1950). In my usual state of impoverishment, and needing to finance my share of the trip, I sold the family pearls to a delighted Parisian jeweler for five hundred dollars. They were worth far more than that, but I was now bartering them for adventure. I didn't give it a thought, not even pausing to wonder how my parents would react to this dastardly deed.

Mike and I managed to return safely to Paris after a movie scenario of a month's trip into Germany, the Soviet zone of Austria, through Trieste, on to Belgrade and Zagreb, including a trip down the famed Yugoslavian coast on a rustic cattleboat with our traveling companions, all Communist partisans. We discovered later that one of the travelling companions who joined us, a Brit who worked for BBC Radio, was really an MI5 British intelligence agent. He mysteriously disappeared within Yugoslavia right after we left and never came home again. Another of our new friends, the enchantingly funny head of the Sputnik tourist bureau, was somehow "eliminated" by the Communist authorities, probably because of his close bonds with Mike and me. It is better not to think about that for too long.

To end this tale, my parents were justifiably furious with me when I eventually returned home without the pearl necklace but with a plethora of really great stories of the unusual trip. If I had to do it all over again, I would, of course, have gone anyway, although it would be wonderful today to play a grande dame in the pearl necklace!

*W*omen have a long history of donning men's clothes. It was a calculated shocker when George Sand, the transvestite writer, dressed like a man in nineteenth-century European society, but then

Coco Chanel put women into masculine trousers, shirts, and sweaters, and people got used to it because women of great taste dressed that way. In this country, famous actresses like Katharine Hepburn and Marlene Dietrich dressed brilliantly in a masculine style, and by the 1960s, when Yves St. Laurent launched "le smoking" (women's dinner jackets just like the men's), the shock value had almost completely disappeared. Bolstered by the women's movement, the trend continues to this day.

As for conservative men's clothing, the accessories today keep things from looking boring, and "the Suits" still dominate in the world of big business. "The Suits" and the relaxed, hip dressers seem to be running on parallel tracks, heading for the same destination, so women can take their pick among those two influences, or they can opt for the third one, the always-present fff styles (feminine, frilly, or fluffy).

Taste in Menswear

Like everything else in the twenty-first century, people are pressing for change in their clothing. The conservative English tailoring taste is being chipped away at by Western European and Hong Kong tailors who are doing their own designs as well as knockoffs.

Beginning in the '50s, leading women's wear designers spent big fortunes launching their menswear collections. It's convenient but still surprising when you can shop in a store today and step into either the men's or women's Armani boutique. Often they carry the same style for both sexes. The CEO of a Fortune 100 company was asked for his opinion on the increase in unisex apparel he was seeing at his headquarters, including women's suits identical to the men's, sometimes the belts, shirts, and neckties, too.

"I don't want to see a beautiful woman wandering around in pajamas she purchased that are just like mine," he said emphatically. "And I sure as hell don't want to see a man wandering around in my wife's nightgowns!" That was his personal opinion on unisex, even though he was addressing the boudoir, not the office!

The way a man is dressed means everything to the way in which he is perceived. A man of taste pays attention to the details of his attire: the length of his jacket, the type of buttonholes, the pattern on his braces versus the pattern in his tie, the buttons on his sleeves, the kind of shoes he has chosen to wear with his business suit or his sports attire, his socks. Everything is of importance to his total look. A well-dressed man inspires confidence. He's disciplined, clean-cut, reliable.

Most men have three wardrobes: spring-summer, fall-winter, and sportswear. Woe unto the man who ignores a private club's dress code. His gaffe is just as conspicuous and humiliating as a woman's would be. Appearing in the newest pair of pastel summer shorts, cotton shirt, and sweater from Paul Stuart's, but pairing this sporty ensemble with his black leather dress business shoes and black socks is one example.

A man's options are endless. Should he wear a pocket square or not? Should he choose an unvented jacket, a single-vent jacket, or a double-vent jacket? Should the jacket have two buttons or three? Which of the three basic types of shirt collars does he prefer? Does he go for French cuffs on his shirt and the obligatory cuff links? Does he look like Cary Grant when he's all through dressing himself?

Away from the office, men have an entirely different set of options. Sportswear for men only developed in the 1930s, when people realized that business suits looked inappropriate in casual settings.

But as soon as men donned shorts and polo shirts, clubs and hotels started legislating how men should dress around the swimming pool, as well as on the golf course and tennis courts. I asked one member of Palm Beach's Bath and Tennis Club how people would react to a male guest who didn't know the rules and showed up in a string bikini.

"That man would be dead," he replied, "and so would the club member who brought him."

Fashion guru Alan Flusser, author of *Clothes and the Man,* proclaimed that men should never wear matched sportswear ensembles or overly aggressive plaids. His advice to men: find out what's appropriate for the settings in which you find yourself, then add a personal touch. "Do what's proper and make it your own." If Cary Grant and Fred Astaire could always do it, then why can't anyone? (A tip for potential wearers of flowers in the buttonhole: a flower pinned to a lapel looks terrible. Have a true buttonhole made on your jacket lapel. Then it can hold the blue cornflower you snitched from a centerpiece, or the best man's lily-of-the-valley boutonnière, or your grandfather's tiny buttonhole American flag.)

Flusser believes that blended suits should never have more synthetic fibers than natural ones because natural materials are soft, luxurious, cool in summer (they allow perspiration and body heat to escape), and warm in winter.

The ubiquitous baseball cap has captured the love and devotion of many American males for decades, but a cap is not to be worn in the house! Some youths insist upon being "capped" at all times, which does not lend a tasteful touch to the interior of a host's home, a theater, or a house of worship, particularly at weddings and funerals! And sitting down in restaurants and cafeterias with a cap on will cast a grown man into utter darkness.

Formerly a gentleman always removed his hat inside the home and office. In fact, he never wore it inside the building. Today's young kids find that absurd, but as we notice the reappearance of more fedoras in winter and straw boaters and Panama hats in summer, perhaps men's hats will embellish our landscape once again and the old rules for removing hats indoors will return. An eighteen-year-old told me defiantly, "That's not going to happen to me and my friends. I take my cap off when I'm in the shower. That's the only rule I follow." He reflected for a second and added, "I might take it off in a hospital."

There's a war of taste raging at present over those who promote as much facial hair as possible on a man, or at least a seven o'clock shadow, and those who feel that scraggly beards, goatees, and extended sideburns will never land in the "good taste" column.

Once upon a time, it seemed as though the Englishman's tailored look, made popular by the Duke of Windsor and others in the royal set, would dominate men's fashions forever. I remember after World War II, when shortages ruined the export-import market, and the men from the Mediterranean countries had to develop their own style, such as tight pinched-at-the-waist jackets, pointed black leather shoes with built-up heels, and dark striped suits that made them look to us Anglos like gamblers and loan sharks. Today a well-dressed, savvy Frenchman, Italian, or Spaniard dresses like any English duke or Irish castle owner, in beautiful tweeds, cashmeres, brogues and laced oxfords, fine shirts, pure silk ties and pocket handkerchiefs, except, of course, when the young, as in the United States, are demonstrating or attending a rock concert.

Fashion Icon of the Century: Jeans

It is fascinating to watch how a fad will take hold and continue ad infinitum (some would say ad nauseam).

Probably the biggest and most enduring fad of this era took off more than sixty years ago. I first became very aware of denim blue jeans at Vassar College in the '40s, simply because everyone else had begun wearing them. Before that time, jeans rarely left the ranch, the farm, or the factory, but once they did, people never looked back.

In the '40s, Levi's had not yet been made for the female body, and the fit was pretty bad. (It was an excellent reason for wearing a big loose white shirt, preferably one's father's, outside one's pants.) My mother came to visit me at college one day, and when she saw me wearing men's jeans with a man's shirt hanging outside, she rued the day in 1873 when Levi Strauss began making these utilitarian garments for the working man. By 1940 blue denim had become the symbol of fashionable casual coverage for Americans of both sexes, rich and poor. Cowboys wore them, and that was sexy enough for both sexes to want to follow along. The Greek toga and the Japanese kimono may have endured for many more centuries, but it appears now that denim jeans will beat every other national garment in popularity and longevity.

Jeans acquired a reputation for symbolizing individualism, rebellion, and the epitome of "cool." The hips and thighs are highlighted in jeans, and today the cut for women allows the wearer to expose the navel and perhaps more below that.

By 1997, most rodeo performers were wearing Wrangler jeans, made with wide belt loops to allow their leather belts to pass through, and higher pockets to prevent the cowboys from having to sit on their wallets astride their horses. Today, celebrities and people with causes like to wear jeans to show the public that they're just regular "plain folks," which is hard to believe when designer jeans can cost up to a thousand dollars a pair! What began as humble denim pants and jackets became more expensive with each passing decade as well-known designers began to include them in their new seasonal lines.

For the world at large, it seems that jeans are the perfect fashion choice for anyone who doesn't know what to wear. They do not require creative decisions except in the choice of jean cut and the accompanying top. Jeans themselves have gone through many transformations—bleaching, darkening, dyeing, or tearing and shredding. As long as the wearer thinks she looks slimmer and more long-legged, she'll wear them. But from this writer's point of view, "tasteful jeans" is an oxymoron.

. . .

*T*oday, our young managerial society may be returning to more formal, well-groomed standards. Somewhere between the two extremes of looking like a well-wrapped birthday present or like a refuse container on the corner on pickup day, there lies a happy medium, where people try to look the best they possibly can but don't suffer emotional distress over a less-than-perfect wardrobe. Somewhere in the mishmash of fashion directions telegraphed to us all day long, thanks to our computers, BlackBerries, iPods, TVs, newspapers, and magazines, we manage to make our wardrobe selections. If we shop at reputable stores or online with reputable companies, if we take the advice of someone with a good eye who will tell us the truth about how we look in something before we purchase it, we will be helping to improve America's taste.

Makeup

A woman of taste has to pass through early adolescence to adulthood in order to learn how to use cosmetics to enhance her looks. It helps to have had older brothers, as I did, who ridicule any use of cosmetics on their sister and therefore keep her from overdoing it. Then, too, I had the Sacred Heart nuns guarding any excess of vanity in their students at the convent. To say the nuns had an iron grip on our appearance at school is an understatement.

I remember how proud I was to have been chosen by the nuns to sit at lunch next to the visiting Reverend Mother Superior, head of the Sacred Heart order in America, an awe-inspiring title. I was thirteen and had persuaded a friend the Saturday before this great event to secretly purchase for me a set of false eyelashes, which my mother would never have allowed. I hid while putting them on at home in the bathroom mirror, but obviously I had not practiced enough. During lunch on this exciting day, as the cream of pea soup course was served, one of my improperly glued eyelashes slipped off and landed in the middle of my soup plate. I stared at it in horror, unable to move. Reverend Mother saw it and thought it was a large cockroach. She grabbed my soup plate and rushed into the kitchen, startling everyone in the room, particularly the sisters working in the kitchen. A cockroach in the soup at the Duchesne Academy head table?

I had the presence of mind to tear off my other eyelash, hide it in my uniform pocket, and pray no one had noticed anything. I'm sure the fallen eyelash met a sudden, violent death at the hands of the nuns in the kitchen. Why I had ever chosen to experiment with such frivolity on such an *un*frivolous occasion, I'll never know.

Women known for their taste apply makeup artfully to look as natural as possible, even while highlighting their best points. There's a world of difference between a beautifully made-up woman's face and a face that stands out as bright as the chorine's in the front row of the chorus line.

THREE

Go, See, and
EDUCATE YOUR EYE

H

IGH SOCIETY in America, as we know it today, began with the robber barons and their wives, and their new wealth. The social arbiter Ward McAllister and Caroline Astor drew up a list of "the 400," what they considered the most important names of society, all of whom were to be invited to the Astors' ball. These people of money and taste were immediately labeled as bona fide members of New York society. Those who did not find their names on the list considered themselves to be totally ruined. Suicides were reported.

The newly rich and social sent their daughters to Europe to absorb refinement and, with luck, to snatch a husband with a title. It didn't matter how great a title, as long as it sounded nice and couldn't be proved a fake. If he married a rich American girl, the titled husband was guaranteed a life of unrelenting pleasure and tea parties in return for his purchase of a wedding ring.

The William K. Vanderbilts were among the most famous of the new 400 in American society. After building a mansion in New York they took the next clever step—hiring renowned architect Stanford White to build Marble House, their "summer cottage" in Newport, Rhode Island. The fact that White accepted their commission meant that they were "made." But there was unfinished business for William's wife, Alva—a foreign title in the family. She needed a titled husband for her daughter Consuelo to establish the Vanderbilt wealth and social power. The number-one title available in Europe at the time belonged to the bachelor Duke of Marlborough. Alva proceeded to force her daughter into a very unhappy marriage, but the wedding festivities would be described for the next fifty years as the "Wedding of the Century."

American women who followed Consuelo's activities wanted to dress like her, carry themselves in the same aristocratic way, decorate their dinner tables in the same manner as the duchess's, and wear long oriental pearl necklaces and chokers just like hers, which was not in the realm of possibility. Even if they had the pearls, most women could never acquire Consuelo's long, swanlike, aristocratic neck, though some young hopefuls attempted neck pull-up exercises, which simply did not work. Nor could they sit as gracefully poised as she on a sofa, listening to the conversation of important but boring men by the hour, and pretending to be fascinated. She was truly the Jacqueline Kennedy of her day.

The taste of the young Vanderbilt heiress was considered infallible. There were as many ambitious mothers at the turn of the century as there are today, but they had a tough row to hoe, trying to turn their daughters into Consuelo Vanderbilts!

Tastes change. Four generations later, half the women in America wanted to look and be like Jackie Kennedy, and the other half wanted to look and be like Marilyn Monroe. They were only exercising their taste, after all.

Ask Your Eye

If you care at all about developing taste, remember that the trick is to train your eye. Every time you enter a beautiful space, ask yourself why you think it is so beautiful. It can be a very pleasant game to play. If you train yourself to stop and think often about what lies behind your perceptions of people, places, and things, you will begin to notice details, pick up the interaction of personal chemistries, and home in on the most important factor of what you are seeing, feeling, or even remembering.

Someone with limited means can develop a sense of taste by training his eye. It is not a Herculean project to train the eye, but it requires an awareness of the subject. It calls for homework. In other words, it's like following the professor's command to "Stay awake while I'm talking to you!" You might, for example:

• Peruse several decorating magazines each month (*Architectural Digest, House & Garden, Veranda, House Beautiful, Elle Décor, Better Homes & Gardens, Real Simple,* and other top publications that cover many topics).
• Become familiar with the names of the leading

architects, interior designers, and manufacturers, as well as the terminology of design. The other day I overheard a lawyer shopping for wallpaper and asking to see the "trump the oil" patterns everyone was talking about. (*Trompe l'oeil* was what she really meant, but the salespeople thought she was referring to Donald Trump and were very perplexed.)

- Glance at the great illustrated design books available in most major libraries. If something catches your eye, read on.

- Use some precious spare time to attend museum lectures on design and architectural trends. Sign up for an adult extension course on the decorative arts. Keep watch for museum tours and lectures in your town so that you won't miss special exhibits on furniture, textiles, and room decoration.

- Visit the "decorator show houses" in your area, which inevitably offer some good design ideas you can use in your own home.

- If your taste is contemporary, don't miss the annual International Contemporary Furniture Fair, held in New York. It is America's answer to the International Furniture Fair in Milan. For the trade only, it is open to the public on its closing day.

- Check out the days on which the furniture marts

around the country are open to the public: Chicago, Atlanta, Washington, Los Angeles, New York, Dallas, and so on. In these places, you will see the newest in home furnishings trends, arranged in spectacularly beautiful room settings to show the merchandise at its best. You'll see the subtle and not-so-subtle changes in the world of home furnishings.

Your curiosity and passion for learning should never abate, even with age, because the pursuit of proportion can be a constant source of joy available to you all through life. Whether you are in a car, on a bus, or walking down a city street or a country lane, what you are looking at is immaterial. Keep those eyes open, observe people, study things of quality in stores and boutiques, and read, read, read. Put yourself in past civilizations, whether you are visiting a museum, reading *National Geographic,* or watching movies about other cultures, present or past. Study our civilization in present time, don't just live in it. Try to notice first what seems pleasing to your eye. Look at a woman who is absolutely beautiful and attempt to analyze just why. Take note of her manners and personality, not just, as television judges, the excellence of her "boobs and butt."

Visit every art show in your vicinity this year; you will be enriched every time you go. Ask yourself, when you're in the midst of an Andy Warhol exhibit, how someone who painted cans of Campbell's tomato soup could be lauded as a great artist. Sit down on a museum bench, stare at those paintings, and consider what made those cans so special. The artist found them fascinating. You may find them just plain weird. Then after some minutes of quiet contemplation, it will come to you that there is a starkness to the composition; there are vivid contrasts in the colors of red and white. The soup cans take on an almost metaphysical glow that you might not have noticed before. It doesn't mean you have fallen in love with a tin can, but you might feel that you now understand this form of contemporary art.

An important part of training your eye is to drop in on every museum or gallery in your vicinity every few months, even if for no longer than fifteen or twenty minutes. There will always be something new to excite your eye. No matter what is on display, it is always of interest to someone. It could be baby clothes of the nineteenth century, weaving in the Amish country of Pennsylvania, or Goyas on loan from the Prado in Madrid. Go see. Even if you do not respond emotionally to anything in that museum that day, take it all in anyway and be able to talk about it. If you take the time to stop, look, and analyze, you'll begin to notice why certain things merit the attention of your eye, just as other things don't.

Allow any library in the world to inspire you. Peruse the illustrated books on artists whose works you happened to see and admire in a magazine. Perhaps it is the field of textiles or stained-glass windows or Indian pottery that fascinates you. It doesn't matter. Whatever holds your attention and draws you in will train your eye. That's how your sense of taste will develop, making you intelligent, selective, and able to respond to beauty in any form.

I have had the great good luck of being educated one way or another every day on the job. The first thing I learned when I graduated from college and finished my graduate work is that I knew absolutely *nothing.* It was a humbling experience but a necessary one. On my first job in Paris, I became acquainted with the best *antiquaires* in town, because Ambassador and Mrs. David Bruce took me many times to the Left Bank antique shops. After examining certain pieces of furniture, silver, or porcelain, the ambassador would teach me why one object was of good quality and another was not. David Bruce was a connoisseur of eighteenth- and nineteenth-century France; he was able to look at the bottom part of a repaired drawer of a *semainier* and tell by the wood whether it had been repaired in the eighteenth, nineteenth, or twentieth century. After these expeditions, my head was usually drowning in a jumble of terms: *cabriole* leg, *fauteuil, faites à la main, tissu de velours, coton imprimé, chinoiseries, passementerie, toile de Jouy,* and *bronze doré.* I faithfully inscribed all the terms and their definitions in my little notebook. I went over them until I had memorized them, and have experienced the joy of recognizing the details of French decorative arts ever since.

In Rome it was like enrolling in a new university. With so many museums to see, newly excavated Roman ruins to explore, and multicentury cathedrals to wander through, my head became glued to the back of my neck from constantly looking upward. The views of the great frescoed ceilings were always the most exciting.

Ambassador Luce was a tough taskmaster. I worked six full days a week, sometimes seven, starting at 8 A.M. and going until 9 P.M. most days. But every free moment I spent continuing my education in the history of art. Wernon, the Luces' private chauffeur, would whisk me to a cathedral, gallery, or ruin if I had even forty minutes free. Ten minutes to get there from my office at the ambassador's residence at rapid speed (in those days, speeding tickets were not handed out to cars with diplomatic plates), fifteen minutes to see what I could see at a sprinting pace, and ten minutes to return to the Villa Taverna.

I was fortunate to become familiar with the showrooms and ateliers of the Italian artisans. Ambassador Clare Boothe Luce had arrived to find an empty embassy residence in need of everything from linens to garden lanterns to china, crystal, and stemware for entertaining, and from pots and pans to dog beds for her miniature toy poodles. I went shopping by the hour, accompanied by an older, wiser Duchessa Lante della Rovere, who taught me the idiosyncracies of buying on the Italian market. The FBO (Foreign Building Operations) purchased the really expensive things—oriental rugs, lighting fixtures, and sterling flatware. The Luces themselves purchased what the house needed and what FBO could not buy—such as a full set of garden furniture for the many lunches and dinners out of doors in the magical Roman climate. What an experience—to have an unlimited budget to purchase only the best for the huge Villa Taverna, the embassy residence. I learned about the great Italian products newly returned to the market (artisan shops had been closed during the war)—items like Murano glass, Venetian lace, Fornari porcelain (*molto* chic), Etruscan pottery, Italian silk fabrics, and Gucci's Florentine leathers. I felt as though it was I who was giving the great dinner parties, to which guests were summoned with the finest papers for invitations, place cards, menu cards, and even Florentine gold-embossed leather table charts that the butler showed to guests at the entrance of the dining room, before they took their places at the tables. All these details were important. The first female American ambassador to a major country, particularly a country like Italy, had to make a *bella figura*!

Tiffany & Co.

Then suddenly it was the spring of 1956, and for a multitude of reasons, I had to come home and start to work in my own country. It was not easy to come back. I had no idea what I was taking on in my new job as the first woman executive at the staid old male bastion of Tiffany's, the leading jeweler, silversmith, and stationer in the world at that point—not just in America.

My new boss, Walter Hoving, often called "the Merchant Prince of New York" because of the length of his résumé as head of the major high-end retail stores in America, considered himself an expert on the subject of taste, and frankly, few would dare to disagree. Taste and good design were uppermost in his thoughts. When he was chairman and CEO of Tiffany & Co., he wrote and lectured constantly on the subject of taste and organized seminars with the leading experts in the field of design.

Although Hoving was head of the Fifth Avenue Association, his passion made him an advocate for taste everywhere in Manhattan. One year during the holiday season, he criticized recent embellishments to the Seagram Building, the latest great creation of Mies van der Rohe. He accused the building management of besmirching the taste of New York by putting up garish Christmas decorations on the famous building's exterior. (Those were the days of bright-colored tree lights, blinking on and off rapidly, and shreds of tinsel hanging like spaghettini from the branches.) "It trashes New York," he sputtered, and, of course, the decorations were removed at once by the Canadian owners,

Bronfmans, and replaced with fresh Christmas trees of varying heights, illuminated by tiny white bulbs—a simple, pure, and beautiful look that was new and yet old European at the same time.

And Hoving was right, always right. I learned more about design during the five years I worked for him in New York than I ever could have learned in forty years of design school.

One day, early in my career at Tiffany, he overheard me talking to a china buyer in the executive circle of desks on the fifth floor. I was offhandedly referring to a low-end store that had opened on Fifth Avenue as an "emporium of tacky taste."

"Miss Baldrige, wrong! There is no such thing as tacky taste!" He intoned emotions like a preacher at the height of his passion, and I wondered, Oh Lord, what terrible thing have I done this time?

"You are absolutely wrong!" he bellowed again at me from the other side of the executive circle. All the other executives working at their desks stopped whatever they were doing and listened. I thought I had infuriated him by criticizing another store on his sacrosanct Fifth Avenue. Instead, he was chastizing me for my viewpoint, something that was to occur with frequency during our professional relationship. When Hoving was mad, he was *mad,* intimidating everyone from the freight elevator attendant to his outside directors. "There is no bad taste!" he repeated, "no atrocious taste, no cheap taste. There is only *taste,* and it implies good, never bad. Otherwise, the word may not be used. If something has no quality, use any word other than *taste.*" Whether Walter Hoving had borrowed this attitude from Van Day Truex, the former president of the Parsons School of Design and Tiffany's new consultant on design development and purchasing, or whether Van had borrowed the attitude from his boss, no one ever knew.

Van Day Truex opened my eyes permanently wide on the subject of taste. A slim figure in constant motion, he glided swiftly through the store, dapper in his highly polished black English oxfords with gray woven patterned socks, a custom-tailored dark gray suit, a pale blue shirt with a highly starched white collar, and a satin damask tie. Van's suit jacket was occasionally adorned with a blue cornflower in the buttonhole. The Tiffany salespeople were simply in awe of him.

One of the young sales assistants on the china floor purchased an artificial cornflower for the buttonhole of his own gray suit, wanting to emulate the master. When Van saw him, his face visibly lost color. He whipped out his wallet, gave the young man five dollars, and sent him off to the florist for a fresh cornflower. "Never an artificial boutonnière," he intoned. "Never!" In his quick travels around the store he would grab from the display counter a newly arrived, just-unpacked porcelain bowl, examine it closely, and then, with the grin of a Michelangelesque angel, he would exclaim into the air that this new import was "only divine, absolutely divine!" The heavens had just delivered a judgment of taste. If Walter Hoving happened to be standing next to him, the gravitas and authority of their joint pronouncements of good or bad were biblical in importance. I liked to follow Van around like a worshipful puppy. He basked in my admiration and explained, taught, questioned himself out loud, put a finger to his chin while he pondered a point, then answered his own question, and came to a decision. *We like it, or we don't.* It was always the correct answer. He got rid of entire lines of famous traditional china because they were "boring." He brought in examples of new shapes, patterns, and sizes from everywhere— Italy, Finland, England, the People's Republic of China, France, Spain, Portugal, and Germany.

In 1956 a whole new Tiffany's was born because

Walter Hoving purchased the store and transformed it. It had been the dowager queen of the carriage-trade stores since 1837, sitting on its precious corner at Fifty-seventh Street and Fifth Avenue, full of the same types of merchandise it had always carried. Tiffany became a textbook of beauty and taste in the gold, silver, flatware, china, and crystal trades. Van and Mr. Hoving got rid of the huge glass display cases full of china or crystal that had lined the aisles of the selling floors for a century. These cases had lent each floor the flavor of a trade show of coffins, and, of course, they had to go.

In the new layout, the merchandise was artfully arranged in specially lit display cases, just like department stores. Other merchandise was shown off to its best advantage in place settings on a table laid for dinner for four, six, or eight. Before, there were only piles of this and stacks of that, representing the store's stock, much like a display of cereal boxes in the supermarket. If you bought a dozen plates as a wedding present, you took them right off the big stack on the table and gave them over to be wrapped and shipped. There was no mystery or romance whatsoever. In the new Tiffany's, with the coffins gone, there were antique dinner tables and chairs, set on beautiful antique rugs. The *antiquaires* who lent the furniture were credited on small, beautifully lettered cards. The finest linens were used on the tables, with centerpieces of fresh flowers and greens.

Table Settings as an Art Form

It was magic. New York's leading society hostesses asked their friend Walter Hoving to let them design table settings, using Tiffany merchandise of their choice, but bringing in their own precious possessions—perhaps a set of eighteenth-century Chinese export trade porcelain or the Vanderbilt family silver service or champagne glasses from a pre–Civil War plantation or the Brussels eighteenth-century lace banquet cloth used in "great-grandmother's house" in Newport. One hostess's portraits of her ancestors were hung on an antique painted screen serving as a wall behind the table. Another hostess put her grandmother's collection of Victorian sterling boxes on a side table. Another brought in an antique dollhouse and fixed up an enchanting setting called "Tea Party with My Dolls." Later the leading society interior designers of the day, such as Mrs. Archibald Brown, Bill Pahlman, Sarah Jessup, Ellen McCluskey, Jimmy Amster, Sister Parish, Billy Baldwin, and the other greats of the latter part of the twentieth century, asked to do tables. They were "allowed to" by Walter Hoving. The results were creative showstoppers. Six months after the first table-setting show was launched, every major store in America was following the idea; it was a whole new area of taste. Crowd of gawkers filled Tiffany's because they could see snippets of the inside of the socialites' and designers' homes. People who lived in Texas and California viewed photographs of the tables in their newspapers or in the shelter magazines. A whole new creative dimension had suddenly been added to the field of entertaining and home design. For people of wealth and taste, there was no more just "throwing" grandmother's tablecloth on the table and using great-grandfather's towering sterling candelabra in the center.

People came from all over America to see the tables and read about the provenance of the items, as well as the family histories of those who had used these beautiful items down through the ages. In the process, they learned a great deal about this aspect of the decorative arts. It was also entertainment because some of the settings were amusing and far-out, such as "Dinner in a Moonlit Forest," "Waffles for Lunch on a Miami Cigarette Boat," and "Breakfast for Three in Bed" (the third person was the couple's child).

We really enjoyed listening to the *oohs* and *aahs* of the visitors who came to see the exhibits—people who had never before cared about or even thought about the subject. I overheard a young bride on a strict budget say with longing, "I never would have thought of combining a black-bordered contemporary china pattern on a gold corduroy tablecloth with black napkins, but it looks wonderful, and someday, when I can afford it, that's what I'll have!" She was definitely in the process of training her eye.

I thought my own eye had been sufficiently trained by my parents and by all those years of work in our embassies abroad, always in beautiful surroundings, with the finest of furniture, antique rugs, tablecloths, china, crystal, and silver to use in official entertaining. I was wrong. My boss, Walter Hoving, called all of his executives together shortly after I joined the staff in the spring of 1956. "No one here knows enough about the things we sell. None of you knows enough about the decorative arts. You don't know the history of the china designs or the powerful influence of the Far East, or the way

people of the aristocracy have lived for centuries."
(If he were giving this same speech to his executives
today, he would have said, "You know nothing
about how the newly rich live.")

As a result of this sudden outburst of criticism,
we were all sent to school. I was lucky to enroll in
an evening class on the decorative arts taught at
the Metropolitan Museum. But before attending I
protested to Mr. Hoving, "I don't really need that
class. I have been working with exquisite things in
the decorative arts during my years as the ambassador's assistant in France and Italy. I have spent a
lifetime in the great museums of the world!"

"Miss Baldrige," he said, "you in particular need
to learn more about the merchandise. You know
about one-half of what you need to know in order
to do a good job publicizing our merchandise."
Ouch!

And he was right. That course, given by Professor Carl Dauterman in conjunction with Columbia
University, opened up a whole new field of knowledge while increasing my interest in, and enjoyment of, beautiful objects. I will enjoy the benefits
for the rest of my life.

I wrote the first edition of *Tiffany Table Settings* after two years of table-setting exhibitions. It was my

idea. I had published two books on other subjects. This one was a natural: photographs with accompanying text would showcase the taste of the New York society and the top interior designers who had come to Tiffany's to demonstrate such an important aspect of entertaining. Lee Prescott, Tiffany's in-house photographer, had taken marvelous still photographs in color and black and white. I was very proud of the finished product until Walter Hoving informed me that the only name that counted was Tiffany's, and my name could be nowhere in the book or on the cover. When I called my father in Washington, crying foul, he stated in very simple terms, "Either you resign in protest, as you are justified in doing, or you take your lumps and realize you will have to take many more in life, and just forget it. Think of the education you're getting on this job!" Correct, as always. It was a much-needed career lesson.

And I will never forget Walter Hoving putting on his white gloves every Saturday and sliding his hands down the railings on all the stairwells in the back of the store to see how clean the area was being kept!

.   .   .

A friend of mine from South America was visiting some Washington friends over the 2005 holidays. One day while we were having tea at the Four Seasons Hotel, she made an unexpected comment. "You know, ignorance is not only distasteful, it's very dangerous." These were sober words from a woman of great taste, always beautifully dressed, with a lovely home, impeccable manners, and an unmistakably jet-set life.

I asked her what brought on this assault on such a grave topic, and she said she happened to be in the Arthur M. Sackler Gallery at the Smithsonian Institution the day before and had experienced a kind of epiphany. "I pride myself," she remarked, "on knowing so much about the culture and traditions of eighteenth- and nineteenth-century Western Europe, as well as my own country, but that is such a finite part of the world.

"Then I accidentally saw a golden garment," she continued, "spotlighted in a vitrine all by itself, and it absolutely knocked me out."

"Go on," I said, now realizing what she was talking about.

"I looked at this unbelievable glittering golden garment, cut in an odd algebraic fashion, and I realized it was the perfect garment for a woman who wants to hide her figure faults. But these were for men, alas."

I laughed and said, "You must have seen the exhibition of sixteenth-century imperial Ottoman Turkish garments, mostly from the Topkapi Palace in Istanbul. The *New York Times* reporter Holland Cotter, in reviewing the Sackler show, called the robes 'space suits for giants.'"

"Well, they would have been good for me, too," she replied. "I found it very interesting to learn that the Ottomans rewarded their heroes with silk 'honor robes' instead of medals and decorations."

She continued. "Are you up for my lecture on the Ottomans?" I assured her I was.

"These people, who began life as tribes of no-madic horsemen in Central Asia, later converted to Islam. Constantinople was renamed Istanbul after they captured it in 1453, and the boundaries of their new empire stretched from Iraq to Morocco. Since Istanbul is situated at the point where Europe joins Asia, the city was as sophisticated and art-rich as al-most any world capital. Artists, poets, scientists, and musicians formed their own salons in Istanbul. Sü-leyman I ("the Magnificent," as he was often called) mixed the refinement of the arts in his court with savage and brutal soldiering out on the battlefields of the countries he was determined to conquer."

"I'm so impressed you know so much about the Ottoman empire."

"Don't be," she retorted. "Until this day I have been ignorant about their entire history and the society in which they lived."

Holland Cotter wrote in *The Times* that people were truly judged by what they wore in that society. My friend and I chuckled at this, wondering what future societies would think of us based on the way many of us dress.

A head of nation visiting Istanbul would be given elaborately embroidered silks to wear. If the visitor's country was not all that important, he might rate only a shoddily tailored robe. A man certainly knew where he stood in Süleyman's reign. If he was important, he might be clad in a silk robe with a dense floral pattern or a shiny caftan made of gold-wrapped thread and embroidered with pomegranates. (A visit to a museum can even tell you about the eating habits of a particular nation.) Ottoman big shots might begin their workday wearing a simple beige satin robe appliquéd with rust red waves and crescents, rendered in tiny stitches and an elaborate array of colored threads. In all probability

no period in history boasted more elaborately attired males. (Peacocks indeed.)

I said to my Argentinian friend, "Knowing you, I
bet you will soon be an expert on Islamic culture,
too."

She laughed. "It's going to take some time. I
have a collection of history books to read, and I'm
going to start studying Arabic. The whole subject is
fascinating, particularly in light of recent world
events. We all need to know more about the major
forces in this world."

And it all had begun because she had accidentally
stumbled on a beautifully illuminated golden Ottoman robe in a Washington museum. She had spent
exactly forty-five minutes there, but it was enough.

You may be in a museum doing research for
your company or classwork for school, or you may
just be curious about a new exhibit. Recently a
smartly dressed middle-aged woman was sitting on
a bench near mine in an otherwise empty room of
the National Gallery of Art. We were looking at the
works of some well-known Impressionist painters.

"I just like sitting here," she suddenly said in answer to a question I hadn't asked her. "I'm here
every day for meditation because it's a perfect way to
get away from the office and avoid a big lunch. I sit

in a different empty gallery each day, just to be able to enjoy what's on the wall without a lot of bodies moving around between me and the paintings. By the time I have finished here, I'll move on to the next building. There's new stuff to look at every time I come."

"Does your job benefit from it?" I asked, hoping to get a hint of where she worked and what she did.

"I find that just thinking in this environment keeps me from making hasty, unwise decisions at work."

I happened to be behind her as she left the gallery, and so out on Pennsylvania Avenue I watched her get into a black corporate limo waiting at the curb. I never did find out who she was, but she obviously was someone of great intelligence, and undoubtedly of influence, too. She taught me that one can meditate successfully without being seated in the lotus position on the floor!

We are all works in progress, as far as the training of the eye is concerned, because every day we are exposed to new visual impressions and sensations worthy of safe storage in our memory banks. When someone says, "Have you all seen the fabulous new exhibit on *chiaroscuro* at the museum?" you might feel a bit sheepish, not knowing what *chiaroscuro* is.

This is the time to make a note, even on a paper cocktail napkin, and go see the exhibit. You will suddenly look at the great paintings of the Early Renaissance with renewed appreciation because these Italian artists were the first to envision space and the contours of the face through shadows. They gave us the visual pleasure of perspective, and while you are enjoying that in their artworks, you will receive intellectual satisfaction, which may make you feel secretly smug, but as long as it is secret, there is no harm! Remember the old Fred Astaire–Ginger Rogers song, "They can't take that away from me."

A person who has traveled widely, studied, wandered through some of the world's great museums, and considers himself "done" educationally, like a medium-rare piece of meat, is in trouble. One is never *done* with the study of art and design and all the benefits that flow from it. It's a lifelong commitment and a great joy that endures even if one is immobile and must be pushed about the galleries and auditoriums in a wheelchair.

There is constant movement within the American design field as the world grows smaller and more connected. Everything from African safaris to Mexican flamenco competitions provides fodder for new designs, but so do the patterns studied while looking at cells under a microscope in a lab. So does a study of the leaves on a great oak tree at sunset. Pattern is everywhere, changing in color and shape as the hours pass. Potential inspiration for graphic designs can be found in surprising places: in the study of entire civilizations, from the Hittites to the Mayans, in new art forms in crystal made possible by chemistry, or in new types of building insulation developed to make housing safer. A textile designer may become excited by the patterns on alligator skins, the rhythm of the cylindrical jars of peanut butter coming off the factory line, the designs on the surface of the moon, or the visual pattern of stalks in a cornfield. Shoe stylists may turn to architecture for inspiration, and one desperate hairdresser presented to the press his new seasonal line of hairstyles that resembled photographs of volcanic eruptions. Everyone is looking, looking, trying to draw from the environment some appealing qualities in the design order. Some projects seem to have evolved from dreams, like Frank Gehry's Dancing House in Prague. It looks to many like a weird nightmare, with its bizarre, twisted columnar shape wrapped around seemingly mysterious filaments.

When you're traveling, there is often a small window of time you can use to check out the museums in the area. Making a museum stop wherever you are, for any amount of time, is worth the time and effort:

- It refreshes your eyes and calms your psyche.
- It gives you the joy either of discovering something new or the comfort of revisiting an old friend.
- It teaches you new things, stimulates the brain.
- It relates the past to the present in the most easily understandable way.
- It moves you away, at least temporarily, from annoying problems in your mind. The visit might even offer an intellectual solution or two.
- It gives you endless material for conversation. You can wake up any dead-in-its-tracks group that seems to have nothing to say about anything.
- It poses all sorts of pleasant intellectual challenges for future study. There is always something wonderful to look forward to. "Tomorrow" becomes a challenging, exciting prospect, not a boring repetition of a same-old, same-old lifestyle.
- It gives you the very good news that your brain is still functioning.
- It makes you realize that things may be gone but not forgotten.

- It gives you a sense of power when you realize you can turn away from the bad and the ugly, and toward the good and the beautiful.

If your child complains of never having anything to do on the weekend, present him or her with a list of the different museums in close proximity, taken off the Internet. It's as easy as finding out what films are showing or when local baseball games and ice hockey matches will take place. Who knows—you might really like the experience yourself because museums are incredible *taste shapers.*

As you become more involved in the arts, you may find yourself making more frequent visits to museums. One modern dictionary defines a museum simply as "a building in which objects of historical, scientific, artistic, or cultural interest are stored and exhibited." A more poetic description characterizes the museum as "an enchanter of children, a never-ending source of creativity for adults, and a soothing comfort for those who are aging." That's certainly true, but I believe museums mean even more than that to our civilization. They connect us with our past, open our minds to new ideas and ways of seeing, and promote tolerance by exposing us to different cultures.

The people whose taste I admire most are habitual visitors and ardent supporters of museums, of whatever kind. Just as self-made businesspeople are to be admired, so are self-made enthusiasts of the arts. To be a museum supporter does not imply merely donating big bucks, although that is a very nice gesture indeed. But those who cannot contribute money can offer their precious time. Volunteer docents give special tours, hold classes for children, organize programs, run gift shops, help organize the fund-raisers for the institution, and most important, talk about the museum all the time. People come as a result. Never forget the power of word of mouth.

The greatest thing about living in Washington, D.C., is that history is inescapably all around us. There are so many great edifices—the Capitol, Washington Monument, Lincoln Memorial, and the White House; seventeenth- and eighteenth-century houses such as Mount Vernon, Decatur House, and Tudor Place; and museums devoted to everything from women, children, the craft of spying, American Indians, and costumes of the First Ladies.

My apartment overlooks the big garden behind the Woodrow Wilson House, which is a property of the National Trust. The Wilsons lived there, he died there, and the house is a treasure trove of his era as president and architect of the League of Nations. Friends who serve on the board of an institution like Woodrow Wilson House become steeped in the history of the period. A board member and friend of mine, Midge McCauley, was doing some work there recently and stopped in the gift shop on her way out. She picked up a twelve-inch-tall talking action figure of President Wilson, dressed in his dark, formal clothes, but she was distressed to find that the speech-making mechanism was not working. She and a fellow docent immediately began to search for the batteries on the figure and found themselves having to remove the president's clothes, including the Wilsonian authentic underwear, socks, braces, and shorts. They got down to the bare skin of the figure, suddenly feeling very embarrassed about undressing a stern, dignified president of the United States.

One of the greatest riches of this country admittedly is the large number of very fine museums devoted to a wide range of subjects beyond paintings and sculpture. (Consider, for example, exhibits of crewel work, weaving, model shipbuilding, lampshades, and Christmas cookies.) Museums may be free or charge a modest entrance fee, nothing comparable to what is needed to cover the cost of exhibiting and caring for their works of art. Some of the buildings may be crumbling, greatly in need of refurbishment. No matter what your interests are—old masters, fly-fishing, architecture, fashion, film, gardening, dance, photography, food, or puppetry—our indoor and outdoor museums open up a world of exciting visual experiences and provide information that can change lives and turn bores into interesting people with something to say. Museums teach history and the enjoyment of art to neophytes, and keep on teaching history and art at every point in a person's life.

FOUR

•

The Taste for
ENTERTAINING

*P*ROBABLY NOTHING shows the depth of your taste or the sincerity of your kindness more than your entertaining skills. You don't have to be hosting a table at a white-tie ball. You're already entertaining when you invite someone to sit on your front porch for a sandwich and iced tea, or when you take a client to a baseball game and a lunch of hot dogs and sauerkraut, or when you serve dessert to your weekly bridge group. You're entertaining when you take someone to the movies and a pizzeria afterward, or when you give a birthday party for a child, or when a friend is simply hanging out in your kitchen over a cup of coffee. You're entertaining every time you make someone feel warm and welcomed after an invitation to step into your environment.

Unfortunately, these are busy times, and entertaining is labor-intensive, requiring planning, efficient communication of the details of your invitation, and the preparation and serving of food and drink in the most attractive way possible. A person of taste manages to turn even the most pedestrian event into something special.

Entertaining does not have to be done on a grand scale, but it should not be done carelessly, either. People known for their good taste pay attention to small details, whether they have invited guests just to please them or whether there is a specific goal in view, such as introducing newcomers, saluting someone's achievements, thanking someone for a favor, making new social or business friends, or raising money. Entertaining is obviously one of the most effective ways to persuade people to join an effort for a good cause.

An invitation to a home-cooked dinner is also

an acknowledged romantic ruse employed by single people of either gender. An excellent wine, someone's best attempt at cooking, and the candles and flowers on the table can turn the simplest dinner into an unforgettably romantic event. Speaking of ruses, a woman I know in Seattle "got her man" by cooking dinner for him on three occasions. By the time he discovered she had never turned on an oven and that all of the food had come from a gourmet delicatessen that was on her way home from her office, he loved her enough to forgive her and asked her to marry him regardless. Today, six years later, she knows how to work a microwave.

No one lives as well today as the highly placed people of ancient Greece and Rome lived or, later, as the courtiers did in Europe or the titled members of Florentine society in the Renaissance. During the Dark Ages in Europe, entertaining was basic and primitive at best. *Feasts,* in contrast to the dinner parties of today, symbolized gluttony rather than taste and were often held in celebration of military victories. Table manners were anything but pretty. Guests used their hands to tear enormous joints of meat dripping with grease off the carcass of a roasted animal. Such castle banquets are a far cry from today's dinners to celebrate weddings, new business relationships, and corporate mergers. Just thinking about those early feasts should make us grateful that our code of table manners today is an enormous aid to our enjoyment of meals.

*E*ntertaining is an effective way to accomplish a number of life's goals. Fortunately, it is a field without limitations. Any number of individuals can participate, the party place can be anywhere from a football field or a sandy beach to a large yacht or a rented crystal-chandeliered ballroom—or one's own home. Any size of budget may be involved, the food can run the gamut from a simple dinner of roast chicken to octopus and snails in garlic sauce, followed by champagne sorbet. The "art of entertaining well" applies equally to an intimate gathering and a party for several hundred people. It covers a range of activities—breakfast, lunch, tea, cocktails, dinner, and supper. People may get together for a sports event, a trip to the theater, a concert, art exhibition, lecture, fashion show, or business anniversary. They may gather to celebrate a merger or acquisition, the launch of a new product, or the rites of passage (birthday, christening, bar mitzvah, *quinceañera,* sweet sixteen party, wedding, anniversary). In other words, when three or more people come together for any length of time outside of work, there's a reason for celebration. One doesn't have to look too far to find a pretext.

The de Gaulle Dinner Party at Versailles

Hopefully every one of us has tucked away in the back of our memory banks a *really* great party—something that was a privilege to have attended. My memory is stuffed solid with such recollections, but if I had to choose which one was the most memorable of all, the answer would be the perfect summer's night of June 1, 1961, when President and Madame Charles de Gaulle hosted President and Mrs. Kennedy at a state dinner at the Château de Versailles. It was frankly unreal, incredible, an unfolding fairy tale.

It was the last night of our state visit to France, and our hosts wanted to show their true affection for our president and, therefore, for our country. Pro-American feeling ran high in France during those days. We had entered World War II in the 1940s in time to help defeat the evil dictators.

A very long table had been set in the Hall of Mirrors, one wall of which was a parade of tall glass windows overlooking the great courtyard, and the opposite wall of which was a series of giant elaborately gold-framed mirrors. Mirrors had been a new decorating fad in France at the time Versailles was under construction. Louis XIV had become so besotted with mirrors that he took over the business from the Dutch, who had assumed they would be its owners forever, and who simply watched in astonishment while the French stole their mirrors away from them!

The table was set with the finest of embroidered linens. The flatware and all of the hollowware were made of *vermeil* (silver-gilt), which cast a golden glow throughout the enormous space. Blush pink and peach flowers filled the space in the center of the table, and the thousands of candles that illuminated the gallery turned the room into a magical candlelit garden, reflecting from wall to wall. There were four goblets at each place, receptacles for the superior rare wines that de Gaulle served his very special guests.

The women were all clad in designer ball gowns

of unashamed opulence. Their jewels sparkled like giant butterflies flitting around the room in the candlelight. They had obviously taken from the family vaults all of their great *bijoux* for the occasion. For any woman not owning great "bling," the top jewelers in France were only too happy to lend the best they had. And their "best" was spectacular.

Jackie Kennedy held her own with all of them. Dressed in a Givenchy white satin sleeveless ball gown, she wore long white kid gloves, which she pulled back over the wrists when it came time to eat dinner. The top of her gown was heavily embroidered in sequined flowers. Her chestnut brown hair was piled high in an upswept coiffure, specially designed in her honor for the occasion by the famed hairdresser Alexandre de Paris, in the shape of the morning pastry called a *brioche*. A diamond moon-shaped clip was centered inside the brioche. The day after photographs appeared in French and American papers of Jackie in her white-gloved splendor, telephones in beauty salons were ringing off the hook with women wanting the *brioche* hairdo, and eager to supply their own diamond brooches and diamond drop earrings so they would "look like Jacqueline" at their next important event.

Since Versailles has no large kitchen and the

nearby Petit Trianon did, platoons of waiters hurried across the torch-illuminated grass carrying plates of food fresh from the Petit Trianon's ovens to the Hall of Mirrors, where other waiters then carried the plates to the tables. A corner of the gallery, behind a giant eighteenth-century painted screen, served as the warming and serving area for the food brought from the real kitchens. There were many courses served on delicate Sèvres china and *vermeil* plates at that dinner. Somehow it all worked, a logistical miracle.

As the obligatory and boring official toasts, given back and forth between the French and the Americans, began to wind down, we heard the sweet sound of violins, coming closer and closer. We looked across the courtyard, and on the other side of the Château we saw a string of moving lights penetrating the darkness. The lights were flaming torch lights, borne aloft by liveried footmen, who were escorting the musicians playing in the total darkness, to fetch the dinner guests on our side of the Château. We followed them back, Pied Piper-like, to the newly restored pale blue, gold, and ivory Louis XV theater for a performance of one of the king's favorite ballets, called *Rendezvous*. The musicians performed on their eighteenth-century instruments, the costumes were of the period (and so were the tiny, uncomfortable seats for the twentieth-century guests with their more ample posteriors).

On the ride back into Paris, we passed through acres of the Versailles gardens, the trees having been especially illuminated for us, and the newly restored fountains splashing in perfect harmony to the classical music and the two national anthems piped by loudspeakers through the trees. The entire motorcade stopped as our president and First Lady walked hand in hand up to one large fountain, fronting a view of what seemed like miles of *allées* in the park, and just stood and looked, hand in hand, hardly believing they were now a part of this life.

The entire presidential party felt the same way.

*E*ntertaining is an awesomely important skill to master in life, in anyone's life, for that matter. Regardless of the size of the budget, it is a way to say thank you, soothe someone's anger, impress others with your talents, or simply to enlist others, because of their respect for you, to join in supporting your cause. Entertaining provides the perfect stage to show off a host's genuine leadership abilities.

Some people are natural-born hosts, while others can be completely thrown by the need for planning and attention to detail. If they find the role of host daunting and worrisome, their guests will feel the same way. If, by contrast, they can enjoy their own parties, the food tastes better for everyone.

Good hosts come in all sizes and ages, as well as a range of incomes. Possessing a pot of gold naturally helps, but the intrinsic part of success comes from actually caring about pleasing the guests, making them relaxed, and helping them forget their problems while they are in your care for a few hours.

Some people feel compelled to work feverishly at acquiring this art, but only for social enhancement or to increase their business opportunities. This kind of egotistical motivation always shows.

Hosts or hostesses who entertain with taste are obviously detail-oriented. Even the smallest details of their parties are memorable because the guests' enjoyment and welfare so obviously come first. Take, for example, a dinner honoring a botanist specializing in research on desert ecology. The guest of honor was delighted and flattered by the host's choice of a table favor. At each guest's place there was a small cactus in a clay pot, with a little card attached giving the plant's name and care instructions.

This sparked a spirited conversation around the table as the scientist expounded on the subject of cacti and each guest learned interesting things about the little potted plant sitting above the dinner plate at his or her place setting.

At the embassy in Rome, Clare Boothe Luce often gave each dinner guest a beautifully bound copy of one of her major speeches. It was the greatest kind of table favor. If asked, she would sign the speech and date it. Then one day, when we were organizing a dinner in honor of a UN official who was planning a visit to Rome, I suggested that the ambassador try the speech idea in reverse—print the guest of honor's latest important speech on fine paper and bind it in a decorative endpaper as a memento for each dinner guest. In those days it was an inexpensive project, costing approximately ten dollars per bound speech, including the decorative cover engraved with the occasion and date of his speech. (The UN official, when he saw everyone exclaiming over their table favors, acted as though, in the American vernacular, "he had died and gone to heaven.")

Even with careful preparation and thoughtful attention to detail, a host can face a series of glitches as a party proceeds. In such cases, the goal is to maintain a sense of humor through it all and make your guests laugh *with* you as you tackle these little disasters. One night in San Francisco, I was the guest of honor at a dinner party, and I was obviously not paying attention when the dessert was served. It was a beautiful, towering white swirled sculpture—not a wedding cake, but as carefully constructed and decorated. The waiter set this mountainous creation before me. While engaged in conversation with my dinner partner, I decided to attack the top layer of the three-tiered confectionary masterpiece. With the strength of one of the Three Musketeers wielding a sword, I thrust my knife into the top tier of this lavish creation of whipped cream, ice cream, and marrons glacés, not realizing that the top, made of frosted cardboard and Styrofoam, was only for decoration while the two tiers beneath made up the edible part of the dessert. As a result of my thrust with the cake knife, the entire confectionary surprise hurtled off its antique sterling-silver platter and onto the dining-room floor. It was one of the very worst moments in my life, since guests of honor aren't supposed to do things like that, particularly after receiving very nice champagne toasts. Our hostess began to roar with laughter, so I followed suit, and so did the other guests. The tension in the dining room was broken. We all survived my gaucherie. The hostess brightly said, "Oh, for heaven's sake, it doesn't matter, Tish. I should have put a sign on the top tier saying, 'Fake tier, eat at your own peril.' And don't worry! The chef who made this creation has already gone home. He'll never know!" The butler reappeared from the kitchen with a large bowl and a sterling serving spoon (no stainless steel for this hostess). He speedily scooped up the wreck into the bowl and the party continued. We all had some of the dessert, and why not? This was a very clean house!

"We're Giving a Little Dinner"

Artwork and writing still in existence from thousands of years ago depict the feasts of the great leaders of the Hittites, Egyptian pharaohs, Babylonian kings, Greeks in their Golden Age, ancient Romans, Mycenaeans, Chinese emperors, and the grand rajahs of India, to name but a few.

The women of those times obviously had no access to the recipes for the food served at state banquets or royal receptions, but they managed to make do without advice from Martha Stewart. Today, the media gives detailed exposure to the art of fine dining, including the ingredients and recipes for everything from meals at the White House to what's on board NASA's spaceships. We have really come a long way from our origins, but it is important to remember that protocol was observed even in ancient times. Only chieftains, emperors, kings, and royals could occupy the important seats at table, whether sitting or reclining. Guests knew just where they fitted into the scheme of things by the places they were given around the food. There must have been great confusion about the process.

Today, there is no margin for error at large official functions. There are seating charts showing each guest's place. However, the menus today often become major issues, considering the differences in taste, health problems, and religious restrictions of the guests.

Entertaining was so much easier in earlier days. Very few people needed table manners, so consequently, there really weren't any. Our modern civilization has piled them on top of the dining experience in unwelcome layers.

In the past, protocol decreed that the blade of the knife to the right of the plate was turned inward. This was not for aesthetic reasons, but for safety. The guest of honor, possibly an enemy and perhaps a would-be assassin of the host, would be seated on his host's left. If the sharp blade of the guest's knife was pointed outward, then that person could pick up his knife and make a quick hard thrust to his right, easily plunging it into the host's heart in one stroke. If he were forced to twist the blade from the inward to the outward position, his actions would be conspicuous, easily seen by the host's bodyguards, who could deflect the blow in time. That is why, many centuries later, the sharp side of the knife blade in our place settings turns toward the plate.

When wars were fought centuries ago, the best bowls, platters, goblets, and later on, eating implements were seized and brought home by plundering armies. Naturally the best shapes and designs were copied and often improved upon by local artisans. Their own taste was the guiding force. Because of constant travel and trade, the mixing of cultures resulted in a greater sophistication in the design of tabletop elements. People with a talent and an eye were allowed, or perhaps even commanded, to make artistic and beautiful equipment for warriors to carry into battle, all of it reflective of the majesty and heroism of their leaders. Major museums today house fabulous collections of the helmets, armor, necklaces, spears, knives, and armor for men and their horses. In the same age, there was a desire for decorative objects such as buckles, bracelets, pins, necklaces, hair ornaments, and rings to enhance the beauty of the leading personages and their women. These treasures are still being copied by modern jewelers.

In ancient times, the head of the house would appoint someone of taste to be in charge of the larder and the table aesthetics (a historic housekeeper/party planner of sorts), including the choice of the vessels for cooking, eating, and drinking. Travelers wandering through countries began to notice how others lived, particularly where, how, and what they ate. We must go back thousands of years to find the beginnings of today's full-fledged "tabletop industry," a new profession related to the beauty and comfort of objects of household use.

It might be said that searching for food and drink, along with making love and fighting to possess or defend, were the only certainties in life in ancient times. Perhaps the same is true even today.

*T*he best dinner parties are those without any ulterior motive. They're rare but wonderful. One woman I know used to drive from New Haven down to Maryland in early March to purchase the superb spring corn to serve at her parties. One day I jokingly asked this jewelry-loving woman what was on her Christmas wish list, expecting to hear about Bulgari's latest ruby, diamond, and gold necklace. Instead she answered, "My greatest wish is always to be able to go down into Maryland to fetch the first spring corn, the nicest crabs, or the earliest asparagus to please my guests." When I asked her why she just didn't get the latest vegetables from her local market, she looked at me disapprovingly. "My guests are worthy of special effort."

Her behavior reflects the best kind of attitude. She does not entertain in order to win a contest, amass compliments, or receive a write-up in a magazine as a superior party giver. She gives her guests especially fresh food because she wants to please them.

A couple I know gives frequent dinners in their beautiful house in St. Louis. They are true oenophiles. He stands at the table before each course to present the wine as though he was introducing the new maestro of the symphony. At the end of the meal each guest is asked to take a sheet from a pretty little gold notepad with its accompanying gold pencil (a table favor) and write the name and year of his or her favorite wine consumed or tasted that night. Two hours later, when the party is over and everyone starts to leave, each guest is handed a handsome wine bottle bag to take home—with a bottle of their favorite vintage of the evening. A lovely surprise. That kind of dinner party is not easily forgotten.

*Y*ou can make entertaining easy by calling in a competent caterer or by going to a hotel or restaurant for your party, but a person of taste does not leave matters entirely up to the professionals. There's a certain starchiness in an event organized entirely by professionals, just as there is in a home decorated entirely by an interior designer. A hostess of merit leaves a personal stamp on her party, and "the personal touch" is no cliché. It's a major asset that warms up something that is cold and makes interesting something that is commonplace.

For example, a Wyoming friend gave a large outdoor barbecue, regaling us with the story of her grandfather's special barbecue sauce served on the ribs. She then enchanted us by giving each guest a small bottle of that sauce to take home at the end of the evening. Another woman in Maine hosted a catered seafood dinner in her home in Prout's Neck; the meal suddenly jumped to life when the guests discovered they were dining on a colorful, very special tablecloth—her great-grandmother's quilt from Ohio, handmade in the nineteenth century. A bachelor in Minnesota serving a steak dinner supplied his guests with knives that he had collected from all parts of the world during a long career of military service. Each knife told its own fascinating story, so there was no lack of conversation during that dinner!

A newlywed couple supplied the caterer for their dinner party with the recipes for the favorite dishes they made for each other during their ten years of courtin'. A woman lawyer in Los Angeles, considered by her clients and colleagues to be a drab, dispassionate person, served as a separate course to her dinner guests two spectacular, beautifully decorated platters of vegetables, resembling the Italian renaissance wreaths of the painter Ghirlandaio. She proudly declared, "You are now seeing my life outside the office. I grew every single one of these vegetables in my garden."

The Guest Has a Job to Do

The guest has a role almost as important as that of the host. Guests are supposed to give, not just take. No matter how they feel at party time, they should make the effort to contribute to the group, to help make the atmosphere warm and attractive, which means all personal problems are kept out of the conversation.

These days a rapid responder, a guest who RSVPs quickly, is a treasure, simply because he or she is in the minority. Who's coming anyway? Too many people today fail to respond to invitations. This rudeness plays havoc with party planning. There are guarantees to honor, rentals to be paid for. Sometimes a host must make two or three calls to a person who has been invited simply to find out if he or she will attend. Hosting is not always a happy, cherished role to play.

The guest who arrives on time is a treasure, but that does not mean arriving even one minute early! Arriving "on time" means within ten or fifteen minutes of the set time. A guest who arrives early incurs the wrath of most hosts, who may be frantically rushing around at the last minute. My husband is often still in the shower when the early birds arrive.

I will never forget the UN ambassador from Japan who arrived an hour early for dinner in my single days in my New York apartment. He had the hour wrong. I was in the shower. When the doorbell rang, I thought it was the deli messenger, bringing me the extra ice I had ordered, so I opened the door in my bathrobe, dripping wet, wearing a shower cap. I was terribly embarrassed, but I think the very proper Japanese diplomat was scarred for life!

I've noticed that people who are known for their taste are quick to compliment their hosts on their food, their homes, their art—anything worthy of praise. Particularly their children! This is not specious but sincere praise.

When conversation at a meal begins to slow, if the host doesn't liven it up again, then a guest should. There might be some cheerful news to relate or a guaranteed-funny story to tell. There are voids a guest can—and should—jump in to fill at any party. (Remember the song, "That's What Friends Are For"?)

Entertaining is a great vehicle to prove how calm you can be in an emergency, which is one of the great qualities of a person of taste. Entertaining makes it possible for you to repay a favor gracefully or simply get to know other people in the most relaxed kind of way.

Some people are natural-born hosts, like Lynda Bird Johnson and her husband, Chuck Robb. "Must be in the genes," a Johnson admirer might say. Her father was the president of the United States, and her mother was one of the warmest, most gracious of First Ladies. Actually, I have wonderful memories of the hospitality of all of the First Ladies in my lifetime, from Mrs. Herbert Hoover to Laura Bush. It's been a question for me of great good fortune, of being in the right place at the right time.

Some people make it a definite priority in life to entertain their friends. They're a dying breed, but they certainly stand out in the landscape. Mary and Bobby Haft, who live across the street from me in Washington, seem to say yes to every charity request to use their home for entertaining, but they also mix the interesting VIPs in town with their own friends. At the same time, they give parties for their children, who are now in their teens and often host the parties themselves. We will all be disappointed if the young Hafts do not grow up to continue the tradition of their parents' hospitality.

Mary and David Holt have homes in Alexandria, Virginia, and on the Outer Banks in Duck, North Carolina, and they entertain often and seemingly effortlessly in either place, in any season. They plan in advance down to the last detail so dexterously that Mary occasionally leaves the airport, just back from a business trip, and arrives at her house when the guests for a party are due to appear.

None of this is effortless. It takes a lot of work, but the hosts say that the gratitude of their guests outweighs the effort. That's a nice thought!

Great Sunday Memories

The longer I live, the more I appreciate having been a little girl in the 1930s and having had a bird's-eye view of the "great society" of the Eastern establishment. I began to understand what entertaining with taste really meant while watching one of America's famous dowagers, Mrs. Henry P. Davison, presiding over the traditional Sunday lunches on her estate, Peacock Point, in Locust Valley, Long Island. Her late husband, a partner of J. P. Morgan, had helped found the American Red Cross and was a founder of the American Museum of Natural History in New York.

These lunches were exciting occasions for children, and there was always a gaggle of us seated at the big table, interwoven with the adults. Known for her taste in entertaining, as well as her vigor in fund-raising for charities, particularly the Red Cross, Kate Davison lived in the big house on the estate, and her grown children and their children lived in smaller homes in the Peacock Point enclave. The estate, with its small and large boats moored in front of the terrace, with the tennis courts, stables, and the scene of fiercely contested tournaments—the grass croquet court—were the stuff of F. Scott Fitzgerald's *Great Gatsby*.

The guests at those Peacock Point Sunday lunches in the 1930s and '40s ranged in age from newborns in baskets to nonagenarians. When an infant began to protest unreasonably during lunch or a child suddenly acted up, he or she was whisked out of the dining room by the nanny. These governesses were a very social group in their own right, greatly respected and royally fed in their own dining room off the kitchen. Mrs.

Davison always thought of everything. There were no omissions in her roster of hospitality, for guests and staff alike.

In the enormous dining room, a supersized mahogany buffet table was set with gleaming silver containers of hot and cold dishes, including chafing dishes of the food that was available in wartime (creamed chicken and rice), as well as the treat of delightful fresh vegetables from the Davison farm. I remember the flowers and greenery on all the tables—straight from the greenhouses on the estate. These visual treats were simply nonexistent at that time in the Midwest, where I grew up. Mrs. Davison lavished her tables with giant mums in the fall. In early spring there was a profusion of tall flowering branches—forsythia and pear blossoms in soaring vases of silver and art nouveau glass. At Christmas, displays of fresh holiday greens, holly berries, gingerbread men, and small red ornaments were everywhere. Although, in later years, I observed magnificent holiday displays at the Metropolitan Museum of Art, Henry du Pont's estate (Winterthur), the Radio City Music Hall in Rockefeller Center, and Biltmore Estate in North Carolina, nothing could compare to the annual scene I witnessed at the Davisons' house.

At Peacock Point a butler was in charge of the dining room. He stood behind Mrs. Davison's chair, overseeing two or three serving men and waitresses, all trained to understand—and fulfill, if possible—the mercurial wishes of the small children who would turn down the turkey for a shyly requested bowl of Rice Krispies (snap, crackle, pop!) with milk. The guest list sometimes stretched to forty around the big table. There was always room, come one, come all, and the food never seemed to end. (My brothers, perfect gluttons in my eyes, would refill their plates two or three times.)

Mrs. Davison greeted each guest with the same attention and welcome, and that included the youngest members at the gathering. At times there would be three generations of one family in attendance. Little eyes and ears were alert. Who could measure how much the children absorbed of the fascinating conversation in the dining room? There were always officers in uniform present, and usually a cabinet officer or top Red Cross official. There was always talk of the war and of heroes past and present, among them Kate Davison's son, Trubee, pilot and founder of the legendary First Yale Unit during World War I. There were usually a couple of English children at the table—refugees from the London blitz staying with "Goggy," the children's name for Mrs. Davison, until it was safe for them to return to England.

She delighted us children by taking us for rides in her electric motor car, used only for driving around the estate. It could reach the astounding speed of twenty miles an hour. Goggy would always wear a great black hat, just like the ones Queen Mary used to wear. The thing I liked most about this amazing car was the little vase of fresh roses perched upon a niche in the back corner of the vehicle interior.

This great woman of taste, who treated children with the same loving attention she gave to adults, lives on in the memory of anyone fortunate enough to have known her. She epitomized the spirit of hospitality and grace.

La Vie en Rose:
Entertaining in Paris (1948–51)

When I was twenty-one, working at my first real job, which happened to be in Paris, I had two of the greatest role models in the world: Ambassador and Mrs. David Bruce. They were famous for their taste in everything from their wardrobes to the books they read, from the food they ate to the company they kept—mainly the intellectuals of France who were their friends. Although I learned about giving huge receptions from them, I learned about entertaining on a small, intimate scale as well. Talk about luck. . . .

I decided to dive in and begin hosting my own parties on a junior scale. I had American friends living in France, French friends I made easily because I spoke their language, and friends from many countries in the diplomatic corps. Everyone was thrilled to be part of France at that time as the country was rebuilding itself and at least some people had returned to the luxuries of their prewar culture.

Of course, when you are young, much is forgiven. You have to be rather brash and reckless to give parties in a foreign country in the first place, but if you are developing your own taste, as I was, courage is needed. I had a flat in the Seventeenth Arrondissement, a chic quarter of the city. On Saturday nights and occasional Sunday lunches, when I wasn't working at some official embassy function, I would entertain at home in a most unusual space. My apartment, originally the top floor of a private home, had been used as a practice studio for the owner, formerly a concert pianist. My living room had been his mini concert hall. There were several polished oak steps leading up to the stage; chairs used to be placed, auditorium-style, on the lower level. It was the perfect place for a party. I could buy liquor at an inexpensive price from the U.S. Commissary used by the American military and the embassy staff. In those days, it seemed as though every American tourist looked me up in Paris, and soon I was entertaining friends of friends of my friends' friends. My list of French friends also grew with every cocktail party. These French friends had never before attended a typical American cocktail party. Even the food was new and unusual to them: "PX cuisine"— cheese sticks, Ritz crackers spread with pimientos in cream cheese, and tiny peanut butter and bacon sandwiches. I really enjoyed watching them as they tasted these strange delicacies with a definite reluctance, and then their faces would relax in smiles.

I had brought from America only one piece of furniture—a portable bar, which I set up on my private stage. Some of my guests, after enthusiastically imbibing my alcohol, would forget about the steps leading to and from the stage in my living room. No one was seriously injured from falling off the stage, but fall they did. An American lawyer friend of mine warned me twice after leaving my party: "You've got to take out an insurance policy for your own protection, or else don't let anyone on the stage!" Having the stage and forbidding guests to use it was an impossibility, so I took out the policy.

There was something very romantic and at the same time absurd about that attic apartment on the rue du Conseiller Collignon. The quirky charm of the place was further enhanced by the fact that my little kitchen and my bathroom, bathtub, et al., were in the same room in back. When I was preparing dinner for a date in those years, it made for some very interesting problems. But when you're young and in love with life, there are no unsolvable problems!

I also had one of life's greatest perks in my Paris job. Our embassy chef liked me, and he did everything from cooking my Thanksgiving turkeys (for a holiday that doesn't exist in Europe) to supplying me with his magnificent hors d'oeuvres that were always in "such great taste" that it didn't matter if I ruined my home-cooked dinner.

Any successful host needs to provide good food, but also well-presented food. Milk or cream for the coffee is brought to the table in a small pitcher, not in its original milk carton! A bottle of

Heinz ketchup or a jar of French's mustard for the burgers is not simply plopped down on the table but is served from small, pretty bowls with silver spoons. Cold beer is a delight to the palate, but how much more attractive it is when served in a porcelain or crystal glass stein. A platter containing the main course at a seated dinner should be carefully arranged, perhaps visually enhanced with a few cherries, sprigs of herbs, stuffed artichoke hearts, or greenery of any kind. (Do not do as I did when I was twenty and cooking dinner for four on the Rhode Island shore one summer. Definitely not a gardener or a hiker, I decorated a platter of sliced meats with sprigs of freshly picked poison ivy. I had considered the sprigs of three leaves by the side of the road to be very decorative.)

It is very gracious of a host, in spite of the fact that she drinks only decaf because of insomnia, to offer her after-dinner guests a choice of either decaf or the real thing. I saw the romance of the evening disappear at one beautiful Fifth Avenue apartment when the hostess sat down after dinner on a sofa covered with a lovely new yellow-flowered fabric from Schumacher. She measured the proper amount of coffee from a jar of Chock Full o'Nuts instant decaf into each antique Meissen demitasse cup.

Then she added hot water from a sterling-silver pot and stirred each little cup as though she was preparing her breakfast cereal. How easy it would have been, in that luxurious household, to have silver pots of deliciously hot coffee and decaf prepared for the guests in the kitchen.

I became aware of the mystique of entertaining in my youth (during the Depression era) just by watching the care with which my father organized his stag Saturday lunches, held bimonthly, with a menu of corned beef, buttered rye bread, mustard, sauerkraut, and beer. His lunches had a political purpose—to further his own congressional campaigns or to help someone else who was running for office. There was so much laughter, joke telling, and bonhomie around the table in the dining room that my brothers and I were able to witness first-hand successful business entertaining. There may have been a specific goal for each lunch, but the pleasure it gave all those men was enough reason.

In that era my mother worked equally hard to please her friends, giving what seemed like endless tea parties, with a friend pouring tea and coffee at each end of the dining-room table. (It was considered a social coup to be asked to pour at these affairs.) Inviting guests for a dinner or luncheon was prohibitively expensive at the time, so tea parties became fashionable. There was always a white antique lace tablecloth with small matching napkins, and the silver was shined to absolute brilliance. (A tarnish mark was considered *disgraceful*.) There was always a bowl of fresh flowers in the center, flanked by sterling candlesticks (the traditional wedding present to the bride from a relative). The food was always pretty to look at, with paper-thin, crustless savory sandwiches, cheese straws, sour-cream-filled celery stalks, deviled eggs sprinkled with the obligatory paprika, and small fresh flowers serving as a border for plates of petits-fours and small sugar cookies. There was always a heavily frosted layer cake, such as coconut meringue. Even at four o'clock the shades would have been pulled down to make the dining room dark enough to warrant candlelight. The hostess was hatless, but any guest who was a lady wore a hat, which she would keep on during the entire party. The rest of her attire could be unremarkable, but if her hat was stunning, she gained the approval of her contemporaries.

In the Depression years, the Midwest was really

hard-hit. In Nebraska we were truly part of the Dust Bowl, with burned crops, locust invasions, and much more. There was little formal entertaining, but I watched my parents make sacrifices to reach out to their friends. I saw the gratitude that was returned and the close bonds that formed as a result.

My mother would gently remind me of what made certain people stand out in their entertaining. "Did you notice those lilacs from Mrs. Gallagher's bushes floating in crystal bowls down the center of the table? . . . Did you notice what a nice toast Dr. Davis gave to everyone at the beginning of the meal? He said something nice about every person sitting around the table, including you children. . . . Did you look carefully at the way Mrs. Miller was dressed tonight? She was wearing hostess pajamas, made of velvet, and those were silver fox cuffs on the sleeves. Very glamorous." (Of course, my mother then had to explain what *glamorous m*eant.) . . . "Wasn't that thoughtful the way our hostess left the table to help old Mrs. Wentworth during dessert? She realized that Mrs. Wentworth needed to go to the bathroom, and so she made sure she could make the trip safely. Letitia, that's what good hostesses do, remember that. They think ahead and solve a problem before it arises." When I was older, of course, I went to dinner parties by myself, but I kept hearing my mother's voice all through my life, reminding me of what it means to be a lady and how important it is to be selective in what you wear, what you say, and what you do—everything done with taste, of course.

People of taste punch up their parties with a touch of the unusual. You can hold an old-fashioned barn dance in a real barn, complete with antihistamine pills for allergy- and hayfever-prone guests. You can host a party at an ice rink, serving hot chocolate made from a prizewinning recipe and featuring a mini ice show with professional skaters. You can hold a dance in the great entrance hall of a historic mansion or hold a wedding on top of a snow-covered ridge (with lifts to get those who don't ski up and down the mountain). Just remember to plan carefully for all contingencies, even the ones you can't possibly predict. (I will never forget one amazing friend who put on the invitation "In case of inclement weather, the location of the garden party will be shifted to the Willard Hotel." On the day of the party, the weather was somewhat inclement, and the host's telephone was out of order. As luck would have it, fifty of the guests went to the host's home and the other sixty went to the Willard. Smart hosts:

they were prepared at both places with an identical menu of food and drinks. They shuttled back and forth between their guests at both venues. Expensive, but so very thoughtful!

The great thing about entertaining is that it does not require a purse of gold, just a will and an ability for hard work. A college senior on a tight budget can still give a memorable party. The hors d'oeuvres may be limited to cheese, Triscuits, and raw vegetables with a store-bought dip. A young couple may give their guests bottles of beer and burgers perfectly grilled in their next-door neighbor's backyard. They lace the burgers with Worcestershire sauce and serve them with fries on paper plates, accompanied by a keg of beer. When they step up in the world, then they can provide perfectly poached salmon with small cucumber sandwiches, served by the pool on sterling-silver trays with Dom Pérignon champagne poured into Baccarat crystal glasses.

It certainly is easier to be a good host when there are ample funds available, but the basic ingredient of fine hosting is in going to the trouble of inviting guests in the first place and actually caring about them in the second.

The composition of the guest list is as important as the food. To invite someone who has suffered a family tragedy and to seat that person between two cheerful, sensitive guests is a sign of the host's kindness. To seat a "pretty young thing" between two elderly people shows a kind heart, provided the young person has been briefed in advance on his or her job to bring cheer. And to seat a person of any age with a knowledge and language skills of a foreign country next to a visitor from that country shows common sense.

Karen and Denis Lamb of Arlington, Virginia, have an impressive supply of different champagne glasses from their years of living abroad. On the way into the dining room when dinner is served, each guest chooses his own glass from the tray of individual glasses sitting there, all of different colors and shapes and decoration. It's fun, and it makes what's in the glass taste even better.

•

Tasteful

SURROUNDS

*I*N ONE major respect, it doesn't matter if you live in an efficiency apartment or a palace, because it's "home," the most special space of all. It's where we hang our hats, examine and reexamine our dreams, make love, and soothe our children and needy friends as well. Home is usually just plain *wonderful,* with all its quirks and faults, just like human beings. It is our space. It adjusts to our moods. It is the basis of our security.

Many believe that living with someone else's taste, as in a marriage or a roommate situation, is the most difficult part of the equation. A prime example is life in a furnished apartment, where one has to accept the decorating decisions made by others. While many people find such setups trying, there are some, often of the male sex, who pay no attention to the possessions around them. For them, a chair is a chair, and the difference between an easy chair, straight chair, corduroy-covered cushion, polka-dotted boudoir chair, or vinyl settee is immaterial. "It's something you can sit on."

In medieval days, the illiterate people of Europe (and that was most of the population) learned about religion and history by studying the interior design of the buildings. Stained-glass windows of cathedrals brought to life scenes from the Bible. Giant tapestries hanging on castle walls re-created valiantly fought battles, with victorious kings, knights, and saints. As ancient frescoed walls, stone forms that were probably used as furniture, and mosaic tiled floors are unearthed and excavated, we are learning that home has always been the center of inspiration for art and beauty for the people of any society. What we put into this special space called home results from the combination of our taste, our exposure to the outside world, and financial resources. Today some people frankly care more about their automobiles, travel plans, cyberspace capabilities, even their wardrobes, than their living quarters. That's their choice, but the rest of us need to come home to a place that pleases, relaxes, protects, and comforts us. It is a priority in our lives.

For many of us, "home" no longer denotes a single place: there's the home in which we were raised and those to which we move through the years as proof of our upward mobility. There's the second home, too, the motor home, the vacation home, and the pied-à-terre in other cities or even countries. There are yachts and floating barge homes, and in today's era of conspicuous consumption, there are now even well-equipped tree houses.

As a natural result of the ever-growing number of newly rich, some people consider signs of wealth to be their number-one decorating imperative. If it takes a palace with inlaid mosaic-tiled floors, gold-lacquered cathedral ceilings, and swimming pools designed for surfing on electronically controlled waves to the musical accompaniment of a leading rock group, then so be it.

Fortunately, somewhere in the middle of all this ostentation, there is a growing, newfound sense of taste and aesthetics. Young people are studying the history of design, visiting museums here and abroad in increasing numbers, attending lectures, and talking—even buzzing—about the subjects they study. We could very well be on the cusp of a renaissance of educated taste, a movement in its earliest stages. Like a lovely little garden, it needs constant, tender care.

We should be grateful that we can even have a discussion about taste in interiors: it was only after the eighteenth century in America that such a topic could be part of conversation. Before then, houses in the United States were built as shelter for survival, and furnishings were primitive. There was an impossible abyss between the lifestyles of most Americans and the wares brought to this country by rich merchants and traders from England, Holland, France, and Spain. They courted a public ready to spend its newly earned money.

Along came the Industrial Revolution in the nineteenth century, and the Machine Age it fostered quickly elevated our standard of living, if not our level of taste. Anyone with "a good eye" managed to find beauty in a mixture of antiques and mass-produced, practical furnishings. They could select, combine, delete, and organize the visual elements of a room or a nook or cranny of a house. It was all part of "home."

Sadly, that elusive skill called taste cannot be bought or inherited, even if there is unlimited money behind it. People who don't try to train an eye think that a giant dark green corduroy couch looks perfectly fine when paired with some delicate flowered seat pads on spindly little gold-painted ballroom chairs. They find that heavy purple velvet draperies with gold tassled tiebacks go perfectly well with tangerine vinyl furniture. Gigundo palaces with eight-car garages have been constructed in enclaves like Beverly Hills; Potomac, Maryland; and all over Long Island to house the newly rich stars of the financial, technological, and entertainment worlds. To many, they look like glorified fast-food stops, lacking only the golden arches overhead. Then there is the fleet of boats, as well as the helipads and the man-made lakes that scream to the world, "Look how this person has made it! Don't you dare ever enter through this gate again and invade his privacy, but do glance over at his aerodynamic spa while you're leaving!"

Fortunately, professional design help is not only for the very rich, but for people of modest but rising means. It's essential to someone who wants to improve, downsize, or enlarge his home. There are so many details and aesthetic decisions to make, building codes to observe, and permits to obtain that the layman could drown in mistakes before the dwelling ever rises from its foundation. If you decide on a firm budget and choose an interior designer with taste, the result will be tasteful, but it is essential that the owner of the house or apartment become part of the project. Otherwise, it will be a cold and lonely place when finished. The personality of the occupant of the space is really as important as the designer, that is, if the owner is blessed with any personality. Great Aunt Hattie's hand-knit afghan thrown over the chaise longue in the bedroom, or the owner's favorite possession since childhood—a toy statue of Davy Crockett, with buckskin moccasins and rifle in hand—are the kinds of elements that bring life and nostalgia to a room, warming it immediately to human dimensions.

Of course, books are one of the most important and revealing parts of an interior design project. Some of the McMansions of the newly rich don't have any real books—only the beautifully bound, gold-embossed leather series of fake books to look impressive on the shelves. I saw the library of one zillionaire on a recent house tour. A handsome room it was, with exquisite wood-paneled walls that had been brought over from a chateau in France. Unfortunately, the built-in book shelves were bare except for an occasional stack of fashion magazines and a grouping of paperback mysteries. The house owner joined the tour at a certain point, and I heard her good friend chide her about the absence of books in the library.

"So what do you suggest?" the owner asked her friend in an embarrassed voice. "I mean, we always get a lot of books at Christmas, so I could use those instead of giving them away. But I guess I can always buy second-hand books by the dozen. Others do that, you know."

"Remove the bookshelves," said her friend, "and turn this space into a really good gym. I noticed that the exercise room you've installed is totally inadequate." The problem of what to do with the bookshelves, and the room, was thus solved. Forget about reading. Work out instead.

Another way to personalize a house is to display framed family photos. One interior designer was so desperate to bring life to a four-story mansion he decorated for a client that he brought in photos of his own family gatherings, handsomely framed, to make the living room and library look real for a house tour. The room was photographed that way by *House & Garden* magazine. Five years later, when the designer had returned for a cursory inspection, his family's pictures were still in the frames.

Lord Duveen, a British Tastemaker for America

The people who became the consultants to the possessors of great fortunes had an undeniable influence on the entire culture in America. One such adviser was hired by Henry Clay Frick, who was one of the great industrialists and a leading figure in America's first high-society group, composed of robber barons and industrialists of the post–Civil War era, including Andrew Mellon, J. P. Morgan, Andrew Carnegie, John D. Rockefeller Jr., Joseph Widener, and Samuel Kress, to name but a few. Shortly before World War I, Frick, the Pittsburgh coke and steel industrialist, built a fantastic mansion at Seventieth Street and Fifth Avenue in New York, with a lovely garden for passersby to enjoy. Being a humble man of little education, he needed help in the design of his house, advice on how to furnish it, and a strategy that would allow him to take his rightful place in New York society. If art was the vehicle to accomplish it, then he knew just the expert to call upon: the British art dealer Lord Duveen of Millbank, who moved right into Henry Clay Frick's life and commandeered his bank account. The house was soon filled with a magnificent collection of art and furnishings. Today it is a museum, and the adjacent Frick Art Reference Library is referred to as "the most comprehensive resource in existence on the history of collection and patronage."

Duveen was clever enough to combine the excess of art available in Europe with America's excess of money. An art expert like Duveen would become the friend of these millionaires and would then persuade them that the way to really move up to the level of the British, French, and other European titled aristocracy was to have their homes embellished not just with good art, but great art. Frick himself knew nothing about the subject, but he realized that having his own collection would enhance his reputation and garner respect for his name. In the course of building the collection, he became knowledgeable himself in the field, particularly with Lord Duveen's tutelage. After all, he had the most famous of advisers at his beck and call. Duveen continued in this advisory position for more than forty years.

One of the loveliest rooms in the Frick house was called the Fragonard Room because it contained Duveen's well-assembled series of paintings by the French artist, depicting the pleasant, amusing life at court in eighteenth-century France. He also bought for the room Marie Antoinette's writing table, her chairs covered in Beauvais tapestry, and the fireplace mantel and andirons that had formerly been in La Bagatelle, the queen's little chateau in Paris. Lord Duveen proceeded to purchase a Houdon bust for his patron and then arranged the Boucher Room for the mansion, containing eight panels of Madame de Pompadour painted by Boucher, Fragonard's rival.

Lord Duveen was the interior designer and buyer for the Hearst Castle in Wales and Mrs. Horace Dodge's mansion in America. In fact, he became the inspiration for every American designer who wanted to move in the highest social circles and make preposterous amounts of money at the same time.

He often acted as social adviser to his clients. He told them what kinds of houses to build, what books to read, where to stay when traveling abroad, and what kind of luggage they should be seen using. Image, image, image! He advised them on their jewelry purchases, introduced them to the "swells" of their era, and even arranged their weddings! He taught art history to Arabella Huntington (a famous name in San Francisco) to help save her position in San Francisco society. She had been snubbed by society and was considered low-class. Soon her conversation became peppered with erudite comments and news of the art world, and she automatically climbed several steps up the social ladder. It was all thanks to Joseph Duveen.

I have always enjoyed reading about Lord Duveen because of his great knowledge of art and architecture. Business schools worship him because of his wheeling and dealing in the acquisition of fine art. He truly understood "the art of the deal." His ruthlessness in making deals can perhaps be forgiven because of his enormous talents.

Leave It to the Tastemakers of France

Those who are good at advising people with money on how to use wealth to further their social position are always in demand. The financial world has always coveted its advisers. The rulers of countries have always had experts telling them what to buy, what to wear, how to arrange their palaces, and whom to invite to dinner. Those beneath them socially have always tried to copy them because, after all, the rich and powerful are the tastemakers of their societies.

Logically, many of these style setters have been women, and one of the first we know about was Madame de Pompadour, an extraordinarily gifted woman who managed to keep the King of France happy between the sheets while simultaneously achieving the position of the number-one interior designer at Versailles. She decorated several homes for Louis XV, including her own magnificent Elysées Palace in the Faubourg St. Honoré, where the president of France now lives. She took over the interior design of Versailles with tireless enthusiasm and was soon regarded as the artistic dictator of France. She invented potpourri (now considered a universal fragrance for the home) and took delight in teaching the courtiers how to dress, how to entertain, and how to make conversation. She even arranged marriages. She was "born to shop," and by constantly purchasing *objets de goût* (tasteful objects)—pieces of

Dresden and Meissen porcelain, paintings by Chardin and François Boucher, tapestries, signed furniture pieces, gold snuffboxes, and the like—she launched an entire industry of making and selling what we would call consumer products in eighteenth-century France.

A Great American Woman
of the Design World

Taste was not a well-known word in this country, except for its usage in terms of food and drink, until certain women, pioneers in design, began talking about it. Edith Wharton, who achieved international fame early in the twentieth century as one of the first American women writers of distinction, penned her first novel, *The Valley of Decision,* when she was forty years old. It became an immediate bestseller, and the money she made from writing began to fund her experiments in interior design. She continued writing bestsellers, including my favorite, *The Age of Innocence,* published in 1920. I had the great good fortune to have served as a consultant on Martin Scorsese's film adaptation of the book.

I particularly enjoy Edith Wharton's constant

references in her novels to character, as well as good
and bad behavior. Her descriptions of the houses,
the parties, the mores, and the ball gowns of the
rich are better than those of any gossip columnist
writing today. In 1897, she and Ogden Codman, a
celebrated architect of the time, wrote *The Decoration of Houses,* one of the earliest books on interior
design published in America. It was the precursor of
the decorating magazines and books of today. The
advice in Wharton's book still applies to current
decorating dilemmas—except in such matters as
room size, domestic service, and plumbing.

Wharton had homes everywhere, including Old
New York, two houses in Newport, a Park Avenue
apartment, a Paris apartment, a house in the French
countryside, and a villa on the Riviera. She was
known for her rich, detailed descriptions of interiors
in her novels. Very logical. She had lived in all those
places herself.

She exemplified good taste. Even her gardens were
the talk of the horticultural world. Everything she
touched turned to success (with the exception of her
relationships with men, which usually ended unhap-
pily). She made great choices in matters of taste—in
houses, gowns, objets d'art, stationery, automobiles,
and, most markedly, in conversation. She may have

made poor choices in men, but her tremendous energy overcame her broken heart. She was too busy to let anything push her backward, when all her life it had been *Forward march*.

Wharton's architectural masterpiece was the Mount, her mansion with enchanting gardens in the Berkshires, in Lenox, Massachusetts. It has been preserved and protected and is well worth a pilgrimage to view it today because of the genius of heart and mind that went into it. Beautiful colors, rich inlaid marble, luxurious fabrics, fine porcelains, paintings by old masters as well as eighteenth-century French artists, oriental rugs of great quality, and stunning light fixtures (some designed by Thomas Edison) all went into making the Mount one of the loveliest houses in America ever designed by and for a woman.

Edith Wharton amassed a galaxy of prizes and awards. She was the first woman ever to receive the Pulitzer Prize for Fiction. She also won the Légion d'Honneur, France's top medal, for bravery during her activities in World War I, when she stayed behind in France as most other Americans went home to escape the Germans.

She represented courageous taste, too, in an era when women were supposed to remain unedu-

cated, untraveled, unintellectual, but physically attractive, nonetheless. She did it all, and she has long
remained the person I would have most liked to
meet in my lifetime.

AFTERTHOUGHT

WHAT HAS been considered laudatory in architecture and interior design changes quite naturally, and
in our age of superrapid communication, these
changes come fast. It's logical to step back and consider just where some of these changes in taste are
taking us as a nation.

Take Las Vegas, Nevada. It's the hottest new place
to go and to live. In terms of population, it's one of
the fastest-growing communities in the world. It's

also a cultural phenomenon. It's where the gambling action is, but also many other kinds of action, especially in the field of home furnishings.

In the 1930s President Kennedy's father purchased the Merchandise Mart (all four million square feet of it) on the Chicago River, with a view to making it *the* place for any professional engaged in the design, manufacturing, and sale of furnishings for residences, commercial buildings, even houseboats and airplanes. Joe Kennedy achieved his goal. Almost every leading member of the industry had a wholesale showroom in the Mart, introduced their new lines "at Market" twice a year, and participated in the design seminars produced there.

By the 1980s, the home-furnishings markets had begun slipping away from one central meeting place in Chicago to regional marts all over the country. Many of the manufacturing plants and glamorous showrooms were centered in the area of High Point, North Carolina. Now, in this new millennium, there are regional markets all over the country, but there has been a significant shift to Las Vegas. It has surprised everyone.

In addition to playing home to new markets, great shows, the gambling casinos, and a high concentration of America's luxury stores, Las Vegas has also attracted star architects and interior designers. Giant hotels are springing up there like desert flowers. A case in point: Steve Wynn's Las Vegas Resort Hotel. Reportedly it cost $2.7 billion to build (the Arab Emirates Palace Hotel in Abu Dhabi bettered it, costing $3 billion), and Wynn's hotel is only the sixteenth-largest one in town. It has a 140-foot-tall artificial mountain made from excavated earth and planted with pine trees. There are two fake waterfalls and an eighteen-hole golf course.

Wynn's fifty-story hotel is arc-shaped and glows in the sunset. The low outbuildings clustered around the big tower resemble a mixture of modern Mayan blocks in orange and cream plaster, lumpy concrete, and thin stone veneer. The interior décor sometimes changes seasonally. The marble floors in the lobbies are covered with garish carpets featuring purple and red flower patterns and crude mosaic designs inset in them as well. There are huge flower balls hanging above and hundreds of potted purple and yellow chrysanthemums mixed with red begonias and beige orchids. As of this writing, the guest rooms have dark brown walls, flat-screen TVs, framed Andy Warhol prints, many digital devices, and outsized bathrooms. Absolutely something for everyone.

One of the main activities in the hotel is to fight

the crowds and wait in line to view the Ferrari-Maserati showroom, which showcases Wynn's own Ferrari Enzo, valued close to a million dollars. (I hope that car will never be subjected to a typical rush hour in New York or Washington, D.C.)

For a nice fee, you can visit Steve Wynn's own painting collection, which includes works by Monet, Picasso, Van Gogh, Gauguin, and the like. There are, naturally, great restaurants and a two-thousand-seat domed theater in the round to prohibit any possible feeling of boredom. But, after reading David Littlejohn's report on the hotel for *The Wall Street Journal,* I think the pièce de résistance is Andy Warhol's ten-foot-long triptych portrait of Steve Wynn, made in 1983 from a Polaroid. The first section shows his face glowing in the lucky color of Chinese red. In the second, his face fades into white. In the third, his face is painted gold, with real diamond dust sprinkled over his dark hair. (The religious painters of the Early Renaissance would have been jealous!)

The New York Times referred to Las Vegas as an "ecstatically tasteless city." It could be the wave of the future, if the reverential crowds and the busy BlackBerries and other gizmos recording the sights and sounds of the environment are any indication.

At the opposite end of the cultural scale is the in-

creasing number of young people going to museums on their lunch hour to visit exhibits on, say, the Bauhaus movement, which epitomized clean, controlled, modern designs, an absence of clutter, and a call for restful interiors. Having viewed the Bauhaus exhibit, you may decide you don't care for that style, and that is fine, too. At least you saw it, and you know what people are talking about when they mention it. Just like Las Vegas. And if your taste runs to items at the Williams-Sonoma store or Ikea or Target—that's fine, too. I believe that happiness comes from looking around us and finding the good and the beautiful in our own culture, and choosing to live with that taste. We are lucky in this country. We can have the real thing, the authentic, the incredibly expensive, or we can have the good reproductions with all of the stylistic accents and details for a modest price. It's a free country, so we can have as much of the glitzy, gold-dust-sprinkled look as we wish—or none of it. It can't be said too often: we are a fortunate nation.

*I*t's hard to begin or conclude a book like this. The author is required to deal with many choices

that are not his own. He should be constantly querying himself, "I think this is terrible taste, but do others feel the same way?"

The eye is the secret of it all. The eye sees what's within its range, in relation to nothing else, or in relation to everything else, including the climate, atmosphere, time of day, action in the area, the people and creatures also present, and one person's mood and memories of the moment. The eye is going to push you, willing or not, into feeling a certain way about what is in front of it. If what you see makes you happy, if it fits nicely into the spectrum of your experience at that particular time, celebrate that moment of success, but don't count on too many more like them.

You may have an excess of ugliness before you, but the wonderful thing is that you have the power *to change it*. Organize your staff, your children, and neighborhood friends to clean up the litter mess on the street outside. Create a library of new and used books on interior design for commercial spaces, homes, and architects' unfulfilled space plans, and make sure the people you care about are reading them. . . . Organize clothing and household furnishing drives for the homeless, donate to a neighborhood rehabilitation project. Buy some fresh new

lampshades for the decrepit old lighting fixtures in your home. Use new placemats and napkins on your table. Fish through your closets, and give away everything that is wearable and fashionable that you are not wearing. Teach your daughter how to decorate her food platters effectively. Buy university lecture tickets and give them away to intelligent high school students. (Make sure they use them!)

In all of these projects, you will be making a more attractive environment for yourself *and others*.

You will never be able to measure the strength of your own personal efforts in the fight for education of the eye of the masses, but this kind of battle is contagious and grows every year in recruits and effectiveness. Even if you have been responsible for an increase in taste in a minute corner of the world, congratulate yourself! A hundred years from now, there may be people talking about your good taste, as they stand before something for which you are responsible.

Now that's a good thought!

INDEX

INDEX

INDEX

INDEX

INDEX